The Men Behind the Scarf

The Battle of Chop Vum

By P. F. Krause

NEW FORUMS

NEW FORUMS PRESS INC.

Published in the United States of America
by New Forums Press, Inc.1018 S. Lewis St.
Stillwater, OK 74074
www.newforums.com

Library of Congress Cataloging-in-Publication Data Pending

This book may be ordered in bulk quantities at discount from New Forums Press, Inc., P.O. Box 876, Stillwater, OK 74076 [Federal I.D. No. 73 1123239]. Printed in the United States of America.

ISBN 10: 1-58107-346-1
ISBN 13: 978-1-58107-346-1

Table of Contents

Prologue

A group of men gathered at a table, while a few others stood nearby listening and occasionally contributing to the conversation. They were looking at pictures taken over 40 years ago in Vietnam and recalling the events of a particular battle in which they were involved.

I was listening in silent astonishment as I heard the stories they were unfolding.

These were Vietnam Veterans meeting at a Company reunion.

As some were talking tears fell and the veteran had to stop and regain composure before continuing on. Others remained somber while remembering the hardships they had to endure. As the conversation continued, some smiled and even laughed at memories that were not so funny then, but they could see humor in the situation now.

I was overwhelmed with their stories. These men were incredible! I had to know more.

The aging veterans openly shared their stories. They answered any and all questions I had. The experience prompted me to capture their stories, in tape recordings and photos, and save them in a scrapbook. *HILL 283, CHOP VUM, The Men Behind the Charlie Co. Scarf in Their Own Words,* is a replication of that scrapbook which is also being published. I can read their stories over and over, and still I am amazed and awed with their courage and strength. They are truly heroes in every sense of the word.

I have written this book to share some of their experiences at Chop Vum. This story is not meant to be accurate. It is a fictional novel. I have taken the liberty to inject subject matter to fill in the blanks and make the story cohesive. The characters are not real, either. I have made them up to fit the plot.

It is based on a true account, and the sacrifices made reflect the cost of this war on our veterans and their families.

I have learned that each man has his own story. Sometimes the accounts of the same battle are different. This makes perfect sense to me. Each person was in a different place and saw a different view. Also, many years had passed since the battle. It makes no difference to me who is most accurate. The important thing is that each man shared their story.

The events of each day are taken from the men as well as the *Daily Staff Journals* of the 1st Battalion, 52nd Infantry, compiled during the units approximately four years in Vietnam.

I thank all who helped make this possible. My children Mindy, Jenny, and Kristin who encouraged me. Kristin spent hours helping me with interviews and talking with the veterans. Holly Martin, who mentored me and taught me so much about writing. All the veterans who answered my many, many questions at the Charlie Company Reunion and cheered me on.

A special thanks to my husband, Philip, who was my inspiration. I am grateful for his unending patience when I repeatedly battered him with questions. And above all, I thank God for sparing his life in Vietnam.

P. F. Krause

CHAPTER 1

LZ Professional, Northwest of Chu Lai, Quang Tin Province, Vietnam

2 March 1969

Positioned on LZ Professional in the fading light of a hot, humid day, the men of the 1/52 Americal Division, Charlie Company, were awaiting orders to return to the field.

Captain Hawk, Company Commander, had just received those orders. He ran his fingers through his hair as a chill went down his spine. "How do ya tell the men this mission may be their last? Maybe it's better if they don't know." Of course, nowhere in Vietnam was totally safe. Every time you went into the bush, you realized you might not come back. This time they would be dropped into a hot LZ – right in the middle of a battle. Facing the enemy was certain. There would be casualties. No choice. They would follow orders.

He was glad no one was close enough to hear him. He hadn't meant to say that out loud. Captain Hawk sat in silence to collect his thoughts. As dread coursed through his veins, he no longer noticed the heat or any of his surroundings. Concern for his men was foremost in his mind. The reports he had heard from Alpha Company to Battalion headquarters painted a dismal picture of where they were going.

Hawk took a deep breath. It was time to meet with the platoon leaders. He looked toward his men that were gathered around their bunkers. Most of them were kids just out of high school. At age twenty-seven, he was considered old. His parents were pleased when he had enlisted in the Army, following in the footsteps of his father. After completing his officer training he took Mary as his wife. A year later, he served his first tour in Vietnam. Now he was back on his second tour, leaving Mary behind with his two children.

He took long strides as he approached the meeting area. You could see his muscles strain against his fatigues. Although his fawn-colored hair was starting to curl up by his collar, he maintained the professional look of a man in charge. The way he carried himself demanded respect. His stomach was in a knot, but no one would know that by looking at him.

It was dusk when Hawk briefed the platoon leaders and squad leaders on their upcoming assignment. "Alpha Company was sent on a reconnaissance mission to report the activity of the NVA. They went in southeast of Camp Tien Phuoc and became completely surrounded. They're running out of everything – food, water, ammo. And men. In the last seven days ten birds have been shot down by the NVA – supply choppers, gunships, and even Medivacs. Camp Tien Phuoc is receiving mortar attack several times every day. The situation is desperate. Bravo Company was sent into the area two days ago, but so far they have been unsuccessful in reaching Alpha Company. We're being sent in to try to join Bravo Company and relieve pressure on Alpha Company. Then we're to continue on their reconnaissance mission."

Hawk pointed to the areas on the map where Alpha and Bravo Company were located. "We'll be going five klicks southwest of Alpha, at the base of Hill 283. Have your men at the helipad by 1200 hours tomorrow. Tell 'em our mission is to help Alpha, Bravo and the Special Forces Camp at Ten Phuoc. The NVA is moving in there, and the camp is in danger of being overrun. Be sure the men load heavy with ammunition... let 'em know we're going into a hot LZ."

Sergeant Ken Merdis looked at his best friend, Sergeant Clark Turner. Merdis had recently become the platoon sergeant. Since he was the most senior squad leader in the third platoon, Hawk had asked him to step up when their platoon leader had been sent to the rear for medical reasons. Clark Turner had taken over as squad leader. Clark's courage in battle was unmatched. He seemed fearless and remained calm under pressure. Merdis saw Clark's clenched jaw. His eyes were narrowed and hard, indicating he was ready for action. "Same shit, different day."

Merdis kept quiet, but he knew it wasn't the same. Clark might not admit it, but he realized this mission would be worse than most. Going into a hot LZ, being scared was inescapable. Even for Clark.

Unknown to the soldiers or headquarters, the NVA had sent in several battalions of 500 men each. South of Tien Phuoc they were making preparations to launch an attack. The Tien Phuoc Special Forces Camp was being used as a diversion while they were making preparations to attack Tam Ky. Tam Ky was a US Army base located twenty miles east of Tien Phuoc. The NVA camouflaged bunkers with plenty of overhead cover to protect the high ground in the area and dug tunnels to aid in moving about unseen. The plan was to repeat the Tet Offensive, in which the North Vietnamese caused considerable damage to the South Vietnamese and US Forces just a year earlier. When military intelligence received information indicating the NVA was infiltrating the area south of Camp Tien Phuoc, they sent Alpha Company in just north of Hill 283 to do recon on NVA movement in the area. That was on February twenty-fifth. For the last five days Alpha Company had been pinned down and were being overrun by the NVA. The men on LZ Professional had no way of knowing the odds they were up against.

Charlie Company had been securing LZ Professional for the last week. On the firebase everyone had to pull guard duty and do odd jobs, which was like a vacation compared with being in the field. While on the firebase everyone got clean clothes, shelter from rain, mail delivery, and ample food and water. They could bathe in a makeshift "shower" made up of a barrel of water on a platform with a hole punched in it — a luxury after being out in the field for a month. It was much safer than being out in the boonies. Since the temperature often registered over one hundred degrees, the men quickly shed their long pants, long-sleeved shirt, steel pot (helmet), and rucksack, and wore only shorts (olive-drab underwear) and their boots.

Professional sat on the higher saddle of a hill. It had been stripped of its vegetation so there would be no cover for the NVA or VC if they attacked. Bunkers were spaced around the perimeter. Each bunker had a structure built of sandbags with four bunks in it. Outside the perimeter were several strings of concertina wire that were laced with trip flares and claymores. If there were an attack by the NVA, the trip flares would alert them, and the men would detonate the claymores.

The firebase was often fired on or attacked, so men were always on watch. Three to four guys were assigned to each bunker and rotated the guard duty.

At LZ Professional the third platoon was assigned to Bunkers twelve through eighteen. Fabe had been assigned to Bunker sixteen along with Lil' Bro, Brian, and Mex. Sitting near the bunker, Fabe and Aloysius Brothers, who he had nicknamed Lil' Bro, were making small talk. In addition to having a last name of Brothers, Fabe looked after him like a big brother would. Fabe was nineteen — only a year older than Lil' Bro — but he had been in Vietnam since November, while Lil' Bro had only been there a month. They were talking about home and enjoying home-baked chocolate chip cookies Fabe's mother had sent from Wisconsin. Because of his handsome features, dark hair, and Fabian-style haircut, he had been dubbed "Fabe". Most of the men didn't even know him by his real name of Joe Bartel. Since joining the Army he had lost weight, but he had never been in better physical condition.

Fabe studied Lil' Bro noticing his curly blonde hair clinging to his forehead, his slight body hunched over, his eyes staring into nothing. He had married young. Now he spent most of his time thinking about his wife and newborn baby boy. Fabe and Lil' Bro hit it off as soon as they met and quickly became buddies.

Lil' Bro pointed to bunker nineteen. "Who's singing?"

"A couple of guys from the first platoon. They're actually pretty good. We call the black guy Ferg. I don't know what his real name is. He's really good on the guitar. The guy with the glasses is CJ. The other guy is Harris — sometimes he sings with them. Those three usually hang around together."

"Where does he keep the guitar?"

"In his locker. Same place you keep your valuables when we're in the field."

"They're pretty damn good."

"Did you listen to the words they're singing? They made their own version of our theme song."

They became silent as Lil' Bro strained to hear the words. He could hear harmony on the chorus of the song.

"We gotta get out of this place
If it's the last thing we ever do
We gotta get out of this place
'Cause man, there's a better life for me and you."

CJ continued with the next verses while Ferg accompanied him.

"Oh man, you're so young and pretty
And one thing I know is true, yeah
You'll be dead before your time is due, I know it.
Watch my buddy out there a-dyin'

Watched the Gooks and NVA, yeah
We been sweatin' and fightin' our lives away."
"We gotta get out of this place
If it's the last thing we ever do
We gotta get out of this place
'Cause man, there's a better life for me and you."

Ken Merdis walked toward bunker sixteen with a purpose in his step. His home was in Oklahoma. He had arrived in Vietnam in September, after being drafted. The men respected him, and Fabe smiled as he approached.

"Want a cookie, Merdis? They're kinda crumbly." Fabe liked Merdis and gladly shared his care package from home. Merdis had helped him more than once since he'd been in Vietnam. Fabe noticed the somber expression on the face of the sandy-haired sergeant standing next to him.

"Thanks." Merdis ate the pieces of the cookie slowly, enjoying the treat. "We're fixin' to head out tomorrow. Alpha Company's in trouble. We'll be flying into a hot LZ. Be sure y'all pack plenty of ammo... you'll need it. Be at the helipad at 1200 hours."

"Tell your mama thanks for the cookies." Merdis headed to the next bunker to spread the word.

Fabe shook his head as Merdis walked away. The companies of the 1/52 often took turns manning Professional. Since Charlie Company had been on the firebase for a week, Fabe wasn't surprised when Merdis said it was time for them to go out into the field. Lil' Bro sat quietly listening. He didn't know what to expect.

Fabe lit a cigarette and walked over to Brian Nelson, who was on guard duty. Sitting on top of the bunker, his big, strong hands held his M60 machine gun. Only one man from each squad had a Pig. The M60 got the nickname of Pig or Hog because its report sounded like the grunt of a barnyard hog. It was also the only rifle that could "huff and puff and blow down houses". Since Brian was tall with broad shoulders, he had been assigned the M60 which was heavier and larger than the M16 rifle that most of the men carried.

Brian kept his chocolate brown eyes fixed on the countryside, scanning the area for any sign of the enemy. He had first met Fabe in basic training. Being from Illinois, he had spent summers working in Wisconsin at a bible camp, so he and Fabe enjoyed talking about home.

"We're headin' out tomorrow."

"I expected." Brian never took his eyes off the horizon. "I heard Alpha Company's in hot water."

No more conversation was needed. They both knew what was ahead.

"You got any cookies left?"

"Yup. I saved the last one for you. It's broken in pieces, but it'll taste just as good."

The mortar platoon was set up in the center of the perimeter. Most of the platoon sat by High Angle Hell, a name they gave their 81mm mortar tube. High Angle Hell could send a mortar round three times as powerful as a hand grenade out to a range of up to 600 meters. It could be calibrated to hit a specific target within that range. It broke down into four pieces – the mortar tube, the tripod, the baseplate and the sight. High Angle Hell, although a great asset to have in the field, took four men to carry. It weighed 89 pounds when fully assembled. They could set it up in five minutes. Everyone, including many of the men in the other platoons carried a high explosive round for High Angle Hell, each round weighing twenty-three pounds.

Whenever they were at Professional the mortar platoon plotted the coordinates for firing mortars into the area outside of the LZ if the enemy attacked. Four men stayed near High Angle Hell ready to fire. Vito Ruiz – known as Rico, "Chief" John Spears, Dan Wallace and "Deadeye" Marvin Holmes were manning the mortar tube. Dan and

Deadeye were from the same town in Arkansas and had been in Vietnam since last May. It came as no surprise to them when the order came to move out in the morning.

Being partly Native American, Chief had an easy-going personality. His smile gave the impression he had no worries. He had dark hair and deeply tanned skin. Chief and Deadeye started cleaning and checking their 90mm Recoilless Rifle. After Charlie Company arrived at LZ Professional a week ago, Captain Hawk had asked for volunteers from the mortar platoon to get special training to operate the Recoilless. Chief and Deadeye had volunteered. They had been training with it the last few days. The Recoilless, a "lightweight" thirty-five pound, air-cooled, single shot weapon, fired a nine-pound HEAT, or high explosive anti-tank, round to a range of up to 450 meters. The tube was fifty-three inches long and three and a half inches in diameter. It could be fired from a bipod on the ground or from the shoulder. It had a site on the top of the tube. They had become comfortable with hitting the targets with the new weapon. At six foot two inches and muscular, Chief had no problem carrying the Recoilless along with his other equipment. Deadeye's job was to carry HEAT rounds and load the weapon. Although Deadeye's small stature made carrying the Recoilless difficult, they went together like thunder and lightning.

"This is a hellava weapon. I think we'll be damn glad to have it along."

"We'll give 'em hell tomorrow, Chief!"

Others from the mortar platoon were sitting in a nearby bunker. Curt Watson, Jr. and Perry "Brooklyn" Fordham had known each other before joining the Army. Coincidentally, they were put in the same unit in Vietnam after being drafted. Not only were they both in the same company and platoon, but even in the same squad.

JR grabbed a deck of cards. "Anybody wanna play a coupla hands of poker?"

"Sure. It's gonna be the last chance fawh a while." Brooklyn pulled up a wooden box for a table and sat on the ground.

"I'm in." Ed Cooper sat down next to Brooklyn. He ran his fingers over his short, ash-blonde hair one way and then the other. He had developed this habit years ago to make his crew-cut look better. Now it had become a nervous habit rather than a maneuver to groom his hair. Since his hair had started growing out, it only served to make his hair look more disheveled.

Brooklyn's mouth twitched as he smiled at Cooper. Although Cooper had only been in Vietnam for a couple of months, he felt as if he had known him for a long time. There was something very innocent about Cooper. Maybe it was his quiet personality, or his baby-blue eyes and pointed little chin.

"Where's Mort? Does he wanna play?" JR asked Brooklyn.

"Uh-uh. He left an hour ago tuh play pokah with Sanchez and Cal."

The guys shortened Dennis Mortenson's name to Mort. He had recently been transferred to the mortar platoon from the first platoon. When Mort wasn't on duty, he often went to play cards with Sanchez and Cal, who were both in the first platoon. Sanchez was a platoon leader. Cal was one of his buddies who had frequently shared a bunker with him.

"He might's well spend time with Sanchez tonight. Once we're in the field there won't be no chance." Brooklyn looked over to Bunker 10, where Mort and Sanchez were laughing.

"Hey, Amos!" JR called out to Amos Myers, his platoon leader. "You wanna play?"

"Naw. I'm gonna write to my woman." Amos said as he stared at the picture he held in his hands.

"You're gonna wear the picture out looking at it!"

"Y'all are just jealous that you don't have a doll waiting

for you!" Amos tucked the picture inside his helmet. He kept it there because it was the only dry, easily accessible place he had when he was in the field.

"She must be some kinda broad, the way yuh always write tuh her." Brooklyn smiled. He had seen her picture — her red hair flowing over her shoulders, her fiery green eyes, her full pink lips.

"Damn right. I only have one month to go, and she's still waitin' for me… I'm about the luckiest SOB there is. We're gettin' married in October, ya know."

"Ya, Ah know."

"Mort promised to be in my wedding. Y'all will be out by then, too, so you guys can come and see for yourself why I write to her every day." Mort and Amos were close. They had met in Basic Training. Amos was tickled to death when Mort got reassigned to Mortars.

Amos pulled out his pen and paper that he carried and started writing.

Dear Judy, Tomorrow we're going out into the field. It sounds like a tough mission, but I'll write a couple lines to you every night if I can. Your love carries me through no matter what we face…

"You're the luckiest bastard I've ever seen!" Mort watched Sanchez scoop up the money they were playing for.

"You're just a piss-poor poker player."

Mort studied Sanchez. His nose, hooked and sharp, cast a shadow on his lips that were curled in amusement. "They probably transferred me to Mortars so you wouldn't rob me blind."

"How'd ya like Mortars?"

"They're a great bunch of guys. I never have to walk point." Mort hated leaving Sanchez' unit, but there was no point in complaining about it. Sanchez was a great leader and possessed a lot of common sense. He treated his men like family. "It's good to be together with Amos again."

"Jeez, Mort! Y'all can talk like it's ok, but they screwed

ya when they transferred you!" Cal shuffled the cards. He snapped the gum he was chewing. His brown, wavy hair took on a red hue from the setting sun. "As my wife always says, "You seem about as happy as a dead pig in the sunshine.""

Mort laughed. Cal was always ready with a saying from Arkansas. "How's your old lady doing these days?"

"Hunkey dorey. She just sent me a shitload of gum. Blackjack, Fruit Stripe, and Doublemint. Want some?"

"I'll take a pack of Fruit Stripe or Doublemint. I never did like Blackjack. Tastes like licorice."

Cal handed him a pack of Fruit Stripe. "I'd sooner have the Blackjack, anyway."

Fabe took over guard duty at 2200 hrs.

Lil' Bro tried to sleep. He wanted to get some rest before they went out in the field, but his mind couldn't shut down. He listened to the roar of the Spooky. The Spooky was an AC-47 Gunship that flew at night. Because it fired up to 6,000 bullets per minute it sounded like a roar and could be heard for miles. It also dropped illumination flares. Each illumination lasted three minutes and lit up the area so the troops could see the enemy moving about in the night. Lil' Bro could see the flares lighting up the sky in the distance. The Spooky induced fear in the enemy. Tonight, it gave the men of Charlie Company a premonition of what they would be facing tomorrow.

After an hour, Lil' Bro gave up on trying to sleep. He walked around the bunker to find Fabe sitting on top. "Everything quiet?"

"Yup. You might's well sit down while you can. Tomorrow'll be a rough day. We're goin' into a hot LZ. That's a place you never wanna go. Charlie will probably be shooting at us while we're landing. The chopper won't touch down if there's gunfire, so we'll probably have to jump off while it's hovering. They won't hover more than

15 seconds. If they do, they're sitting ducks – so we have to be ready to spring into action."

"I'm scared, Fabe."

"We don't have any choice about going out there. Just concentrate on the job at hand. I just do as I'm told and pray to God I'm not the next one out in a body bag. Not all our missions are this dangerous. It's rough when you have to go into a hot LZ."

His voice got very soft, "We're all scared."

Lil' Bro' nodded, sat down, and looked up at the stars. "It's hard to believe it's the same sky we see in Kansas. My wife and I used to sit outside in the evening and watch the stars come out. We'd talk about our son and buying a house. I probably could have avoided coming to Nam. Our folks didn't approve of our getting married so young. Since my family had a strong military background, I knew I had to go when my draft notice came – my family would have disowned me if I didn't. We were only seventeen when we were married. Now she's living with her folks. And I'm here. It's too late now. There's no turning back.

Fabe never took his eyes off the countryside so he didn't see the tears forming in Lil' Bro's eyes.

CHAPTER 2

Hot LZ

3 March, 1969 – 1100 Hours

Charlie Company spent the morning rotating watch duty and getting ready to pull out. Delta Company would come to Professional shortly before noon to take over the LZ. The men painstakingly gathered their equipment and packed their rucksacks. C-rations, water, and ammunition had been dropped off that morning by helicopter. Their rucksacks would weigh sixty pounds or more when they were done packing.

Since Lil' Bro had only gone out in the field once before, Fabe checked with him before heading down to the helipad. "Be sure you have everything."

"I think I do, but let's run through it." Lil' Bro opened his rucksack.

Fabe started to go through the checklist. "Three to four days C-rations – twelve meals."

"I hate the beans with franks and the ham with lima beans, so I left 'em behind."

Fabe laughed. "We call them 'ham and muthas'. Take 'em along – you might be able to trade with some sucker or you might get desperate enough to eat 'em."

"I'll never be that desperate. Do you want the cigarettes and coffee? Or should I leave 'em?"

"I'll tell you what... I'll trade my ham loaf for your teenie weenies, a pack of cigarettes, and coffee."

"Deal." Lil' Bro handed Fabe the 4-pack of Marlboro, coffee, and beans with franks. He considered it a good trade. He liked the ham loaf.

Fabe continued going through the checklist. "Air mattress, poncho, poncho liner, four canteens of water on your rucksack, plus one on your belt. Entrenching tool..."

Lil' Bro interrupted, "What?"

"The folding shovel." He continued with the list. "Insect repellent."

Lil' Bro touched the insect repellent he had placed in the elastic band of his helmet. "Last time I went out I had it in my rucksack. I couldn't get to it to kill those damn leeches, so this time I have it handy."

Fabe smiled. Lil 'Bro was learning. "Extra clips of ammunition in your ammo pouches."

"Got 'em. Plus the two bandoliers of ammunition I will wear. I attached my hand grenades to the straps of my rucksack."

"And a Claymore mine with its clacker and wire."

Lil' Bro looked down at the radio sitting on the ground at his side. "Merdis asked me to carry the radio. I have the extra battery and smoke grenades. That adds thirty extra pounds for me to carry. It's more than anyone else has to drag around."

"Not really. If you don't have the radio, you have to carry a mortar round weighing twenty-three pounds or extra rounds for the M60 machine gun. The mortar platoon has a lot of heavy equipment to carry. It all evens out."

"Boy, the shit I'm carrying weighs more than I do!"

Fabe smiled. "Be sure you have your first aid pouch with the field dressing on your belt. You know the radio call signs, right?"

"Roger. Captain Hawk is Charlie 6. The others are indicated by their platoon and squad. We're 3-2. Since I won't be calling in to headquarters, those are the only ones I'll be using."

"Looks like you're good to go."

"What about soap, toothbrush, comb, clean socks, and underwear?"

"Forget the underwear – no one wears them in the field – it'll rub your balls raw. Take the other stuff if you want to. It's unlikely you'll have a chance to use it – it's just extra crap to drag along."

"Then I guess I won't need my towel either."

"You'll need it to wipe your sweat. It's going to be hotter'n hell out there."

"Okay."

"Sometimes I put my towel under the straps of my rucksack so they don't cut in so much. Where are your dog tags?"

"One around my neck, the other on the lace of my shoe tucked under by the tongue."

"Good job."

"I saw you do that a few days ago, so I figured it must be a good idea."

The temperature was already in the nineties and humid when the 104 men of Charlie Company arrived at the helipad. They had to be ready when the choppers came in to take them to the field, as there would be no warning before the choppers arrived. In less than a minute, the men would be loaded and the choppers back in the air. Four choppers would be coming in at once. It would take four trips to carry all of Charlie Company to the hot LZ.

The men gathered around the outside of the helipad in groups according to the platoon and squad they were in. They were all loaded down with supplies and wearing a black scarf with a red "C" in the corner. Each man in Charlie Company had been given a C scarf by Captain Hawk.

Charlie Company had four platoons – First, Second, Third, and Mortars, AKA Weapons or Fourth. Ideally there would be four squads of ten men in each platoon, except Mortars who had only two squads. In reality, they could not keep enough replacements to reach that level. At this time the first, second, and third platoon had three squads of seven to nine men, and the weapons platoon had two squads. Each platoon and squad had a leader. Captain Hawk competently led the entire company.

Captain Hawk joined his men who were gathered by platoons. He joined the first platoon, since he would be flying out with them. He sat down and stared at his hands.

This was an assignment he was dreading. When TOC gave him the orders yesterday, they didn't tell him everything. But he knew plenty. He had heard Alpha Company call into TOC many times in the last few days. There were several reports that concerned him. He needed to be prepared for what was ahead, so he carefully considered the information he had overheard.

Alpha Company had been inserted near Hill 283, also known as Chop Vum Mountain, a week earlier. They were on a reconnaissance mission. And they certainly had found the North Vietnamese Army. Their reports to headquarters were alarming, indicating there was at least one battalion of NVA troops — or perhaps even headquarters for a major operation. Three of the reports were of particular concern.

First of all, Alpha Company had reported finding WD1 commo wire — wire used for communication in major operations. The troubling part was that after Alpha Company had cut out a three-meter section of wire the NVA had returned to the area a day later and repaired it. The fact that the NVA was monitoring the area and had the resources to replace the wire indicated a major operation.

Secondly, Alpha Company reported the NVA had new equipment. They had new pith helmets and a full complement of ammunition. That was unusual. It suggested they were a very prepared unit that had just come in from the north.

Thirdly, Alpha Company observed an area where the NVA had dug holes in a checkerboard pattern. There was a spider hole in front, a second one behind it to cover the first one, a third one at an angle to cover the second one, and a fourth to cover the second and third one. This was a defense pattern the NVA only used when they were dug in for a major fight.

To make matters worse, the last couple of days Alpha Company had called in several times with horrendous reports. They were getting hammered, losing many men. It was next to impossible to get in resupply. The heavy anti-aircraft fire from the NVA left a number of helicopters disabled or shot down.

Hawk took a deep breath. He surveyed his men waiting for the choppers to take them into the hot LZ. Soon they'd see if things were as dangerous as he had anticipated.

The third platoon went to the north side of the helipad. Fabe and Lil' Bro joined Brian and Carlos Garcia, who most of the guys knew only as "Mex". Mex, a draftee from New Mexico, left a wife at home. He was considered the 'old man' at age twenty-three. When he was in college, he had a student deferment, allowing him to be exempt from service until he graduated.

Fabe took his Hallmark calendar out of his wallet. It was the size of a playing card and had the entire year on it. He had a red circle around October thirty-first. That was when he would leave Vietnam. He put an X on March third. Every day he marked off a day so he would keep track. Another day closer to going home.

Merdis stood at the edge of the helipad talking to Clark Turner. Clark stood slightly taller than Merdis and had light brown hair and a villain's mustache. He carried an M14 rifle with a starlite scope for night vision. He usually had a smile and a joke for his men, but when the going got tough he was hell on wheels.

The men of the third platoon strained to listen to the radio Lil' Bro carried. He had it tuned to the frequency Alpha Company used – everyone wanted to hear updates on the area they were going into. They heard a constant barrage of machine gun fire which nearly drowned out the words.

"It sounds like Alpha is really putting out." Lil' Bro's comment sounded more like a question.

Fabe was listening to the radio, too. "I'm sure they're giving it all they can... you can hear the sound of the AK-47. That's from the NVA. You'll soon learn to tell the difference between the AK-47 and the sound of the M16 we carry."

"Alpha 6 to 1-2."

"Go ahead Alpha 6."

"Dustoff with gunships has been requested. Retreat with wounded to yesterday's dustoff area."

"Roger."

Clearly, there was trouble in River City.

The conversation from the men in Alpha Company set everyone's nerves on edge. Each man handled his fear differently. Mex became quiet. Fabe started polishing his rifle. Clark fell into character and began telling jokes, although only Merdis and Brian were listening to him.

Brian stood up and took his Kodak Instamatic camera out of the side pocket of his pants. He turned the round knob on top to the next number. "Smile! You're on Candid Camera."

Clark smiled, lifted his M14 above his head, and posed. "They told me I was going on a vacation to a tropical paradise with beautiful girls and swaying palm trees. They didn't tell me the girls were going to be in the palm trees shooting at me."

His antics and humor decreased the tension considerably.

The mortar platoon waited on the west side of the helipad. Most of the guys were sitting down talking to each other.

Mort walked up and down looking at everyone, as he did every time they went into the field. Typically, somebody would not come back. Either they would get killed or wounded. Maybe shot. Maybe hit with shrapnel from a booby trap. Maybe hit with a mortar. *Will it be me or someone else this time?*

He looked into each person's eyes for some sign. Nothing gave any indication of what was to come. Then Mort looked across the helipad at the first platoon. When he looked at Cal, their eyes locked. It sent chills down Mort's spine.

His gaze went to Sanchez who was talking to Captain Hawk. Sanchez was twenty-one years old — three years older than Mort. Unlike Mort, he had enlisted. He wanted a career in the Army, following in his father's footsteps. Mort was mighty glad he'd be out in two years.

Mort returned his attention to his own platoon. Amos was looking at the picture of his fiancé. He looked up. His eyes met Mort's. No words were needed. They both realized they might not return.

Mort enjoyed reading Shakespeare, and he thought of an excerpt from one of his plays:

"All the world's a stage,
And all the men and women merely players
They have their exits, and their entrances."

The radio transmission interrupted Mort's thoughts.

"3-2 to Alpha 6." The mortar platoon also had their radio tuned in to Alpha Company's frequency.

"Go ahead, Alpha 6."

"Dustoff shot down while attempting to extract wounded. Seven more wounded, two killed." You could barely make out the words over the noise of machine gun fire.

"Roger. Wait one."

Captain Hawk saw the men's reaction to the radio transmission. "Alright everyone. Listen up! I want everyone to keep their radios on the frequency for Charlie Company. You don't even need to turn them on until the choppers get here."

Everyone got busy doing something. Some talked softly with their buddies, some were looking through their rucksacks. No one mentioned Alpha Company again or the danger they were heading into.

The first platoon was sitting on the east side of the helipad. Ferg was sitting next to CJ and Harris. "Ah hate waitin'."

"Quit your bellyachin'. Look it. See that?" CJ held up his glasses. "Can't see a damn thing. Always steamed up and dirty." CJ wiped his glasses with the scarf from around his neck.

"Why botha cleanin' 'em?"

"It's kinda hard hitting your target if you can't see it."

"What you talkin' 'bout? You can't hit da broad side of a barn, nohow."

"I'm not trying to hit barns. I'm trying to save YOUR ass!"

Harris studied CJ. His pale skin, thin lips and sandy hair brushed forward were a stark contrast to Ferg who had dark skin, full lips and short, kinky hair. Harris smiled. He was a man of few words, preferring to listen rather than talk. He enjoyed hanging around with CJ and Ferg. They were always bickering about something. It was like watching a sitcom on TV. Maybe when he got home he would try writing. It would be a war comedy starring Ferg and CJ. He'd call it Black & White.

Captain Hawk stood on the south side of the helipad by the second platoon. At 1510 hours he yelled, "Choppers in site! Get your shit together! Line up! Second platoon goes first. I'll go in with the first platoon on the second load, then mortars and third platoon."

The second platoon knew exactly what to do. They moved like a polished machine. Donning their rucksacks and grabbing their weapons, they formed lines of three or four men on opposite sides of the helipad.

The helicopters made a deafening sound. They landed between the lines of the men. Without saying a word, the men hopped on from both sides of the choppers. The first two men moved to the middle, the next two on each side sat by the open doors with their legs hanging down. A door gunner also sat in the open door on each side of the chopper. In less than a minute they were off into a hot war zone.

Ten minutes later the first platoon was boarding the choppers.

At 1530 the helicopters returned to pick up the mortar platoon. JR sat next to Brooklyn inside the huey. They could hear reports on the radio from the platoons that were already in the combat zone.

Deadeye sat by Chief and Dan on the right side of the chopper, with his legs dangling out from the chopper. The adrenaline started firing through his bloodstream, making it hard to distinguish between fear and excitement. Chief carried the Recoilless, a 45 caliber pistol, and two rounds for the recoilless. Deadeye also carried rounds for the recoilless. Rico took a position by Cooper. Cooper carried the radio for the mortar platoon. The weight of his pack prevented him from getting up without help if he sat down. Because of that, he sat at the very edge of the chopper by the door on the left side.

As they neared their destination, they could see the gunships firing tracers into the tree line and the other platoons firing at the NVA. There was no way of knowing what to expect. There could be three or four NVA shooting at you or three or four dozen. For that matter, there could be a hundred.

The helicopter pilot leveled his skids nine feet above the water of the rice paddy. None of the men wanted to jump out from that height. The door gunner pushed Cooper out. He sunk into the mud of the rice paddy. The water went over his head. *My God, it's black!* He could see nothing. Out of necessity, he started walking. After two steps, he felt a rise in the ground. Quickly, he stepped onto the rise formed by a dike. Being firmer than the muck he landed in, it placed the upper part of his body above the water. He gasped for air. As he looked around, he spotted some North Vietnamese running at the edge of the rice paddy. He was shaking as he raised his M16, pointed it in the direction of the NVA soldiers, and pulled the trigger. The wet weapon misfired. A feeling of panic grew within him. If they saw him, he was SOL.

He took a deep breath. He had to keep calm or he'd get killed. If he just stood there he was an easy target. Trying to get his rifle to fire, he slapped the magazine to be sure it was in all the way. He fumbled with the rifle's mechanism as he pulled the charging handle back and discharged the cartridge. Praying the rifle would fire, he released the charging handle and it fed in a new round. This time the rifle fired. *Thank God!*

He fired off all the rounds he could, not taking the time to aim. Cooper let out a deep breath of relief, seeing the gooks running for cover. He didn't know if he hit his target, but it didn't matter as long as they were running away.

When Rico saw Cooper get pushed off, he decided to jump. He was fortunate enough to land a few feet from Cooper where the water wasn't as deep.

The door gunner on the other side pushed Deadeye out the door. He sunk into the muck, the smelly water up to his chest. He had barely touched the bottom when the water started jumping around him. Enemy fire came from several directions.

"Holy Shit!" He scrambled toward the tree line to his left without ever looking back at Chief.

Chief jumped into the water feet first. Because of his heavy load he sunk into the mud. The water came up to his armpits. The Recoilless had to stay dry to be useful, so he carried it on his shoulder to keep it out of the water. This made it difficult to keep his balance. He couldn't move his feet. Looking at Deadeye, he saw bullets jumping in the water. Out of desperation, he used all his strength to pull his foot up from the sucking mud and begin making his way to the tree line.

As they neared the tree line, Rico caught up with Deadeye. Chief and Dan closed in on the distance between them. Out of nowhere, a hand grenade came whirling through the air. Chief's eyes grew big. "GRENADE!" If it detonated, they were a-goner.

Without giving it a thought, Rico jumped up and reached for the grenade. The breath caught in Chief's throat as Rico successfully caught it. Without a pause, Rico threw the grenade in the other direction. They turned and ran into the tree line with unbelievable speed, considering their loads.

Anticipating the impact of the explosion behind them, they didn't slow down until they joined the other men — there was no time to think about it. Then they realized nothing happened. Chief stared in disbelief. "What the hell?"

Rico stood there with his mouth open in amazement. Miraculously, the grenade turned out to be a dud.

The third platoon went out last at 1540. Merdis, Mex and Brian were on the left side of the chopper. Clark was on the right along with Lil' Bro and Fabe. Merdis and Clark were last to get on the chopper. Fabe's pulse increased with the staccato pulse of the chopper's blades. Being in the last group was especially dangerous. The NVA would know the chopper would be dropping off the troops in the same spot as the previous groups.

As they neared the rice paddy, the door gunner placed a hand on Lil' Bro's back.

"4-1 to 3-2."

Clark grabbed the handset from Lil' Bro and responded to the radio, "Go ahead 4-1."

"The assholes in the choppers pushed us out at ten feet above the ground."

"Roger that."

Clark moved closer to the door gunner on the right side of the chopper. He unlatched the door gunner's safety strap and put his M14 rifle up to his head. "You're gonna be the first one out if y'all don't get this chopper lower. I don't think you better push anyone on this chopper out."

The door gunner turned around and looked at Clark and down the barrel of the M14. He took his hand off Lil' Bro's back.

As they flew over rice paddies, something red caught Fabe's eye. He tapped 'Lil Bro on the arm and pointed to an object in one of the paddies. Lil' Bro's blue eyes widened as he spotted the helicopter with a red cross on it laying on its side. He looked questioningly at Fabe, but there was no use trying to talk above the deafening thrum of the helicopter blades.

Fabe shuddered. The Geneva Convention forbid firing at a chopper with a red cross. The fact that one was shot down in the area indicated the NVA didn't care about the rules. A new wave of fear passed over him.

Near the area of drop-off, they saw two Cobra Gunships pounding fire into the tree line at the north side of the rice paddy. The men from the mortar platoon were already in the tree line on the south side of the rice paddy.

The pilot lowered the chopper and went down to four feet above the rice paddy before hoovering. "JUMP!"

Fabe and Lil' Bro jumped off and sank in above their knees in mud and water. Unconsciously, Fabe tightened his hands on his M16 in a death grip. He and Lil' Bro scrambled through the water and caught up with Mex and Brian. They followed Clark and Merdis making their way south to the tree line. As they ran, they fired their weapons blindly into the tree line on the other side of the paddy. They didn't even notice their wet feet and muddy pants.

Fabe paused to catch his breath when the third platoon joined the rest of the company. They stopped under the cover of trees at the edge of the jungle to regroup. "Whoever decided to drop us in here had shit for brains!"

"Goddamn right." Mex had stopped next to Fabe.

Everyone checked their weapons, re-loaded, and braced for anything the enemy had to offer.

The gunships followed the choppers that brought them in and were already out of sight.

The men huddled together in groups as their eyes searched the rice paddies and surrounding areas for any sign of movement. Everything was quiet.

Fabe and Mex worked their way over to Lil' Bro and Merdis. Lil' Bro looked scared and confused.

Fabe read Lil' Bro's mind. "That's how Charlie does it…

One minute they are all over you, the next minute they all disappear. You never know where they're hiding, or when they'll hit again."

CHAPTER 3

Hill 283 – Chop Vum

1550 Hours

All was quiet. The eerie silence became unbearable. Lil' Bro had never been so scared in his life… and he had only been here for fifteen minutes. He knew the worst was yet to come. How was he going to survive for a year? He jumped when he heard Captain Hawk bark out orders on the radio. There he stood, like a statue, too dazed to move.

The men formed a tight unit in the tree line, as ordered. Hawk directed them to head southeast for two klicks and find a suitable site for their night lager.

Sanchez, having superior leadership skills in battle, led the way. He cared deeply about his men and made sure they were always prepared. The first platoon was followed by second platoon and mortars. Third platoon pulled up the rear.

It would be dark in a couple of hours, so they had to get moving. Lieutenant Sanchez called out, "Ferg, it's your turn to walk point."

"Geez, Sanchez! Are you flippin' crazy? Ferg's new at this. Let me walk point." CJ said as he went to the front of the line. "I'm the best there is and I've been here the longest."

"Go ahead."

Ferg let out a sigh of relief. Walking point meant you would be the first one to walk into an ambush or receive sniper fire. Although Ferg was closer to CJ than anyone else in the company, he wasn't worried about him taking the lead. CJ was the best.

Harris smiled as he listened. In spite of the bickering

between CJ and Ferg, the "black and white" team always took care of each other.

CJ liked to pull point and often volunteered to do so. It was a dangerous job, but he liked the adrenaline rush. He also knew he was good at it and didn't want to put Ferg in the lead — he just didn't have enough experience for this mission.

Proceeding in single file, the men of Charlie Company headed up a hill through the jungle. CJ's skilled eyes scanned the thick jungle for venomous snakes, trip wires, booby traps, Viet Cong, and signs of the NVA as he chose a path for the company to follow. The least snag of a foot could trip a wire and blow you to hell. He was followed by Ferg, Harris and Sanchez, giving him backup. Cal walked behind Sanchez carrying the radio for the first platoon.

Captain Hawk fell in line with the second platoon. When they were in the field his company headquarters consisted of a sergeant who assisted him, two RTOs, and the forward observer and his RTO. One RTO kept on the frequency of Charlie Company to keep in touch with each squad, and the other RTO kept on frequency of TOC, or Tactical Operation Center, at battalion headquarters.

After the mortar platoon fell in line, the third platoon brought up the rear. Fabe, Mex and Brian fell in place behind Lil' Bro. Since Lil' Bro carried the radio, he would have to stay close to Merdis, who was leading their platoon.

They had barely entered the jungle when they heard a cluster of rifle shots, followed by silence. Fabe immediately dropped to one knee and raised his rifle. Since they were so far behind the first platoon, there was no way of knowing what happened. Because Lil' Bro walked less than ten feet ahead of him, Fabe strained to listen for a radio report. The only sound he heard was that of his heart pounding. His eyes strained to see into the dense jungle, watching for the slightest movement. *Where are they? They could be five feet away and I'd never see the bastards.*

Within thirty seconds, he heard the radio.

"1-2 to Charlie 6."

"Go ahead 1-2."

"Three spider holes, one VC killed, one VC wounded, one captured. Wearing black pajamas. Weapons retrieved."

"Roger. Comin' your way. Keep the prisoner ALIVE. Charlie 6 out."

Fabe let out a deep breath. Obviously, the situation was under control. CJ had noticed the spider holes before the VC were able to take out any men. Thank God they had an experienced point man.

Captain Hawk went up to the front of the line to secure the prisoner and check on the wounded VC. The VC were not part of the NVA but were part of a guerilla force that fought in conjunction with the NVA. They were easily distinguished from the NVA by the black pajama-style clothing they wore.

Captain Hawk saw the spider holes where the three VC had been waiting in ambush. The holes were small enough for one man to fit snugly, then a camouflaged cover went over the hole. When troops got near, the VC in the spider holes would jump up and lay fire on the unsuspecting men.

"Great job, CJ. Most fellas wouldn't have seen those spider holes."

As Captain Hawk approached the wounded VC, he saw him take his last breath. One of the medics was bending over him. He shook his head. Captain Hawk took his eyes off the dead VC and turned his attention to the prisoner.

Captain Hawk questioned the prisoner, speaking fluent Vietnamese. When he was convinced that the VC would not give him any information, he ordered his men to tie his hands and gag him so they could continue on. They put a burlap bag over his head and tied a rope around his waist. He would have to get the prisoner sent back to headquarters as soon as possible for interrogation. Meanwhile, he had to protect him. Most of his men had seen too much death and destruction. They would have no qualms about killing him.

CJ and Ferg moved the bodies of the two dead VC to the side of the trail. "Thanks, CJ. I recon I would'na see dem spider holes. Good ting ya cleaned dem rims dis mornin'. You saved mah life."

"It ain't nothin'. Just keep my back covered… since I can't hit the back side of a barn."

Ferg chuckled. "Dat's da truth."

CJ adjusted his helmet, and they continued on their mission to find a place to form their night perimeter.

Captain Hawk took the prisoner with him back to his position behind the first platoon. He radioed Merdis, and asked him to send up Turner. He waited for Turner to join him.

"Turner! Assign a man in your squad to watch the prisoner. I'm holding you responsible for his safety."

"Yes, Sir!" Clark put the muzzle of his M14 at the prisoner's back. "Didi mau, you mother fucker!"

Since Brooklyn was carrying an M16, he led the mortar platoon. Behind him was their Platoon leader, Amos. He carried the sight for High Angle Hell strapped to his rucksack frame. He also had an M16. Since Cooper was the RTO, he stayed close to Amos. The men carrying High Angle Hell were next. When the men stopped moving, they bunched up together.

Brooklyn had heard the full report on the radio Cooper was carrying. "I'd love to get mah hands on that shit-faced Gook. I'd teach him a lesson."

Cooper turned and looked at Brooklyn in amazement. Would he, too, turn bitter after he was here longer? Right now, all he could think about was trying to keep his feet moving. He felt like a pathetic hunk of shit. With mud from head to toe, the wet clothes chafed his skin every time he moved. He stunk like a compost pile. The radio on his back felt like a hundred pounds. He didn't care one iota about the frickin' prisoner. He just wanted to get somewhere to sit down and take off the damn radio. And dry off.

Mort and Amos exchanged glances. They had been watching Cooper and Brooklyn. Cooper was still green. He didn't feel the animosity the other men did toward the enemy. It wouldn't be long before he understood why Brooklyn felt the way he did. There was only a handful of men that wouldn't kill the VC if they had the chance. However, they would follow the Captain's orders and stay away from the prisoner. For now.

Rico and Dan huddled together. Rico removed his helmet and wiped the sweat off his brow with his shirt sleeve. "God, I hate this friggin' jungle."

Dan looked at the dense foliage around him. He looked toward the sky where the leaves blocked out all sunlight except for a few stray beams of light. He jumped as he heard something snap. He automatically raised his rifle in anticipation of an enemy sniper sneaking up on him. As he turned, he let out a breath of relief as Deadeye stepped closer. "Take it easy, it's me."

"Next time talk to me. I almost blew your head off."

Fabe fell in line when they started moving again. His feet felt squishy with every step. His feet would stay wet – they wouldn't have a chance to take their boots off on this mission. Sweat dripped down his back. He didn't know what caused the sweat – the stifling heat or the intense fear that overcame him. His sixth sense told him trouble was ahead. He hoped he was wrong, but he had learned his hunches were often right.

Brian and Mex stayed right behind Fabe.

Walking single file, the company stretched out for about one-fourth of a kilometer. This left a smaller target if they should be ambushed, but it also meant an ambush could take place anywhere along the line.

The progress went painfully slow. Although the temperature in the jungle felt cooler, the air felt so heavy with humidity it was almost like walking through soup. There was no breeze below the green canopy of trees. Fabe could barely see the man walking ten feet in front of him. The jungle closed in and became dense and practically as dark as night. The leaves above were the size of umbrellas and the sharp vines and foliage reached out at him. Since he only had on his t-shirt, his arms were getting cut up. Moisture dripped off the trees. Fabe felt something on his neck. He touched it with his hand and felt a cold, slimy leech already attached. He grabbed the bottle of insect repellant from the band of his helmet and squirted the repellant on the leech. Immediately the leech fell off. Usually you could not feel the leeches. Somehow they managed to get under your shirt and other clothing. Then you'd find a huge, reddish-black, slimy blood-sucking glob.

Lil' Bro had never been in the dense jungle before. He didn't know what to do. All his training never prepared him for this. He thought AIT was difficult, but it was nothing compared to this. He could see Merdis in front of him. The best he could do was study Merdis — where he stepped, Lil' Bro stepped. The nauseating smell of rotting plants and mud overpowered his senses. He felt like puking — maybe from the smell or maybe from fear. His thoughts raced: *What's next? Where'll we spend the night? We can't stay in this fuckin' jungle! The jungle's so thick, Charlie could be on top of us and we wouldn't see 'em. What'll I do if I see a gook? Will I really be able to shoot someone?*

After an hour of struggling through the jungle, Fabe knew they would be reaching the area of their night lager soon. Maybe his hunches were wrong and it would be a quiet night.

Frrrraaaak! The explosive sound of gunfire shattered the air.

Fabe threw himself to the ground and raised his rifle as the unmistakable crack of the AK-47 and the hissing of RPG rounds sent chills down his spine. He could not see what was happening ahead of them. Brian and Mex crawled on their bellies until they were next to Fabe.

"Holy shit! Sounds like an ambush!"

CHAPTER 4

Ambush

1750 Hours

CJ cautiously made his way through the jungle looking for booby traps, punji sticks, snipers and any signs of an ambush. He sensed danger. Analyzing every sound in the jungle, he heard nothing unusual – mostly silence, with occasional buzzing and chirping of insects.

He swung his rifle from left to right with each step he took. He had the safety off and his finger on the trigger, ready to fire at the slightest indication of the enemy. He didn't know where the NVA waited, but they were out there somewhere. He could almost smell them. They would attack again when they had the advantage. He became so intense – for him there was no other world except that of survival.

Seeing clearing ahead, he gave a sigh of relief. They had made it out of the frickin' jungle. Suddenly the hairs on his neck stood on end. The jungle was totally silent. He sucked in his breath as all hell broke loose. Fire came from every direction, bullets flying everywhere. Pulling the trigger of his rifle, everything went black as he thumped to the ground.

Captain Hawk grabbed the handset of the radio his RTO was carrying and began running toward the front of the line causing his RTO to run alongside him. Seconds later the report he was dreading came across his radio.

"1-2 to Alpha 6!" Cal's voice was loud and hurried.

"Go ahead."

"Heavy fire. Pinned down. Need help. Green uniforms."

"Comin' up!"

The men of the second platoon followed Captain Hawk's

lead as they charged in to give support to the men in front of them.

Brooklyn continuously scanned the jungle around him but saw no movement. The gunfire coming from ahead continued with no breaks. He strained to hear the radio.

"Green uniforms. That means at least one NVA unit. God help us." Brooklyn said, not talking to anyone in particular. Instinctively, he crawled closer to Cooper so he could hear the radio better. Mort joined them.

"Charlie 6 to 4-1."

"This is 4-1."

"We need the Recoilless NOW! Get your asses up here!"

"Roger."

Since Brooklyn and Amos were carrying rifles, they worked their way to the front with Chief and Deadeye. They would give them cover, as needed. They also carried extra rounds for the recoilless. Cooper followed right behind Amos.

Deadeye had an evil smile on his face. "BASTARDS! Y'all kiss my ass! We're comin' to get ya!"

From a small clearing, they could see gunfire coming from the area directly ahead of them. The sharp, acrid smoke made their eyes water.

"Take this, yuh assholes!" Brooklyn laid out heavy fire to provide some cover.

"Piss on you — you ain't the only one who can raise hell." No one could hear Amos over the deafening sound of gunfire.

Brooklyn, Amos, and Cooper joined the first and second platoons in laying out heavy gunfire into the direction of the ambush.

"Over there!" Deadeye started running toward Captain Hawk.

Neither Deadeye nor Chief looked to the side to those who laid on the ground moaning and screaming for help. They had to focus on their mission.

Chief and Deadeye spotted a banana tree near Captain Hawk. They crawled in that direction and positioned themselves behind it. The banana tree reached up only ten feet, but it provided some cover. It sure as hell beat being out in the open.

Captain Hawk pointed. "There, you see them in the tree line? That's your target."

Chief kneeled on his right knee, his left ankle forming a right angle with the ground. Holding his body erect, he gripped the monopod with his left hand and grasped the trigger grips with his right hand. He raised his right elbow to the height of his shoulder, forming a pocket for the bipod shoulder rest. Deadeye took a kneeling position opposite Chief's right shoulder and faced to the rear of the recoilless. He placed his left knee on the ground close enough to Chief so he could talk to him while loading the weapon. "You can do it! Give 'em hell."

Chief took a deep breath.

Deadeye swung open the hinged door on the end of the recoilless and loaded a round. His hand shook as he tapped Chief on the shoulder and moved away. "UP!" That was his signal to Chief and Hawk that he had the weapon loaded and the breech and the backblast area was clear.

Hawk had been listening for Deadeye's signal. "FIRE!"

Chief sighted in. He took a deep breath of air, let a little out, then held his breath. Breathing while firing would throw off his aim. He pressed the trigger safety with the crotch of his hand, slowly and steadily squeezing the trigger, being careful not to flinch. His heart pumped hard against his chest making it hard to stay calm.

The gun roared, sending pieces of shell case out the breech of the rifle, and sending a mighty blast toward the NVA. Everything in the path of the round fell and the area opened up. The round hit part of the banana tree, splitting it. "Son of a bitch!" Chief's only cover had been blown away.

Deadeye immediately moved in next to Chief and pulled

the breach open to reload. He could not take the time to fret over their exposed position. He tapped Chief on the shoulder. "UP!"

A machine gun from the NVA opened up on them. Now both Hawk and Chief could see exactly where the machine gun fire came from. "There!" Hawk pointed.

Without saying a word, Chief took a deep breath, re-adjusted, sited in, and fired another round. This time they hit their target dead on.

Deadeye reloaded.

Captain Hawk let out a sigh of relief.

After Chief fired the fourth round, Captain Hawk could see the NVA had retreated. "CEASE FIRE." *Thank God!*

Chief checked the recoilless. "Get some HEAT rounds from Brooklyn and Mort. We have to have this badass ready."

Deadeye was on his way before Chief finished the sentence.

All shooting had stopped. Brooklyn looked around. Someone was lying twenty feet away just past a thick tangle of brush. He could see the man's blood on his pants and heard him calling for help. Cradling his rifle in his arms, he dropped to the ground, crawled through the underbrush, and made his way to the wounded soldier. He recognized Harris as one of Mort's friends from the first platoon. As he crawled closer on his belly, Brooklyn could see he had a wound in his right shoulder. The blood covering his right pant leg indicated he had probably been hit there, also.

"I can't get up. I can't feel my leg."

Brooklyn looked around. He could see there were a lot of wounded men. Medics from every platoon were busy. He looked back at Harris. The blood was soaking the pants on his right thigh. Brooklyn's heart was pounding, and his mind was racing. *There's so many wounded... the medics are too busy to help me... there could be a sniper anywhere... I feel so helpless... I don't know what to do.* Staring at Harris, his eyes landed on the first aid pouch attached to his belt. He calmed himself as he took out the field dressing it held. Next, he ripped Harris' pants so he could see where the bleeding was coming from. Flesh was torn away at the impact point of the bullet. Blood was oozing in a continual stream. Brooklyn had to do something to control the bleeding or Harris would not make it. He removed the wrapper and put the dressing over the wound. Holding it in place with one hand, he wrapped one of the tails of the dressing tightly around the leg, then wrapped the other tail in the opposite direction. He tied the tails in a knot. When he could see his bandage was helping, he let out a sigh of relief. "That should help the bleedin'."

Harris was moaning and his eyes rolled back in his head as he looked at his right arm, "Oh God! My arm!"

Brooklyn looked up at Harris' arm. Blood was oozing from his shoulder where the tendons were exposed. There was no way he could put a dressing on that. "I'll get you to a medic."

Brooklyn grabbed Harris by his left arm and shoulder, and with strength beyond his own, he dragged him out of the underbrush. JR saw Brooklyn struggling, and ran to help. Together they lifted Harris and carried him to the clearing. "Medic! GODDAMMIT! WE NEED A MEDIC!"

Brooklyn let out a breath of relief when he saw Doc Bauer running toward him. "Geez, Doc! What can I do?"

"Get his pack off. I got morphine. After I wrap his arm you can put him over by the other wounded men."

The men in the third platoon knew the Mortar platoon had made it to the front of the line as they heard the Recoilless boom into action. After the fourth round, the shooting ceased.

"Charlie 6 to all platoons. Second platoon spread out and secure the area. Everyone else up to help with wounded. Leave one squad from the third platoon to watch the rear."

Merdis turned to Lil' Bro, "Y'all stick with me!"

Clark hollered to the rest of the guys. "First squad stay and watch our rear and guard the prisoner. The rest of you – get the lead out of your asses!"

At the front of the line, everyone spread out knowing what needed to be done. Everyone, that is, except those who were cherries, like Lil' Bro and Cooper.

Fabe saw a dark-haired soldier lying prone. He and Mex ran to his motionless body hoping he was still alive. "I can't see where he was hit."

Fabe grabbed his shoulder and rolled him over. His head flopped. On his forehead Fabe saw a circular hole rimmed with abraded skin. His eyes were still open.

Fabe's clenched fist slammed into the damp earth. His jaw was clenched as he looked around at other injured men lying helplessly on the ground.

"Sanchez," Fabe whispered to Mex. Somehow, it seemed more respectful to the dead if you spoke softly.

They knew what to do – it was all too familiar to them. Fabe took charge. "You take his feet; I'll take his shoulders. Lift on count of three. One. Two. Three."

Without saying another word, they carried his lifeless body to an area where others were gathering the wounded.

After completing the morbid task they ran to Cal, who they saw lying partially on his side in an unnatural position. When they got closer, they could see Cal's body was covered in blood. His right chest had a chunk of flesh missing. The area looked deep purple and was clotted with blood. A shiny white area from an exposed rib bordered the wound. Blood stained his shirt, arms, and pants. Blood was already drying in the corner of his mouth. His eyes stared unseeingly into the distance. The radio remained on his back, along with his rucksack.

As Fabe and Mex were removing his pack, Lil' Bro came running over to see if he could help. When he got close, his breath caught in his throat. He swallowed hard, hoping he could keep from puking. He tried to look away, but he couldn't. Standing there motionless, the color drained from his face. Tears were streaming down his cheeks as he mumbled to himself. "I'm not in Kansas anymore."

Fabe and Mex were not immune to the horrific sight, but they had enough experience to know they had to keep moving. You had to shut it out. You had no choice but to move forward if you wanted to stay alive. They quickly picked up Cal and took him to lay beside Sanchez.

Merdis was beside Doc Bauer, the medic for the third platoon. They were kneeling by CJ who had heavy bleeding from his chest. Propping him up, Doc wrapped a bandage around his chest. The blood immediately started seeping through. Thankfully, CJ was in shock. Merdis knew he didn't realize what happened. Doc gave instructions to Merdis, "Keep him upright, or he'll drown in his own blood."

Merdis nodded. "Clark! Y'all get your ugly ass over here and help me move CJ."

Clark ran over to Merdis. "You take his head; I'll take his feet."

"NO! Y'all will have to lock arms with me. Put one arm under his legs and keep him in a sitting position so he can breathe."

CJ let out a moan as they picked him up. Mex ran over to grab CJ's Rucksack and rifle. He paused as he saw the bent glasses laying on the ground. He stood motionless. He thought of last night, as he watched CJ and Ferg singing *"We gotta get out of this place, if it's the last thing we ever do."* Funny how those words struck home now. He shook his head as if to erase that memory. Picking up the glasses, he shoved them in CJ's rucksack, and ran to catch up with Merdis and Clark.

Brian and Fabe joined Mex, Doc Bauer, and another medic who was stooped over Ferg. He was wrapping a bandage around his bloody right leg, while the other medic gave him a shot of morphine. Ferg had been hit by sniper fire just above his knee. After the medics left to attend others, he tried to get up. He let out a grunt as the world started spinning around and he fell to the ground. Mex grabbed Ferg's rifle and rucksack. Brian and Fabe stepped up so Ferg could put an arm around their shoulders as he struggled to stand. Dizziness threatened to overtake his senses, but he grabbed tightly to Brian and Fabe as he hobbled on one leg. Each time his left leg hit the ground he shuddered, but he kept up as he hobbled over to the other wounded.

Ferg pointed to Harris, who was lying on the ground. "Put me by Harris."

"Is that you, Ferg? I thought you were dead." Tears formed in his eyes. The morphine had kicked in, making his pain more bearable.

Ferg was quiet for a minute while he closed his eyes to let his dizziness subside.

"Ah ain't dead". "What 'bout CJ?"

"Don't know. But we're goin' home."

By this time the men who were killed and wounded were put into one area. The wounds had been tended to as best they could do under the circumstances. Daylight was fading fast. They had to find a place to hole up for the night.

In all, four men were killed, and six wounded — all from the first platoon. They had been in the field less than 3 hours.

CHAPTER 5

Night Without Foxholes

1830 Hours

Third platoon and mortar platoon were assigned to carry the wounded and dead. Those carrying the mortar tube and bipod for High Angle Hell were excluded from the duty. Mort carried the baseplate tied to the frame of his rucksack, leaving his hands free to help carry the casualties. Since Chief had the recoilless, Deadeye needed to stay close to him. Second platoon took the lead, followed by mortars and third platoon. The first platoon took the rear.

Brooklyn looked at Mort as they bent to pick up one end of a poncho with a body in it. "I sure as hell hope they made sure these guys were dead befawh they wrapped 'em up. Yuh want I should check 'em and be sure?"

"Good idea... what if?" Mort watched Brooklyn pull back the poncho flap.

Sanchez stared up at Mort with vacant eyes. His face looked like a clay mask, with a black hole in the forehead. His mouth hung open — the smile that was always on his face wiped away in death.

Mort's eyes drifted to his chest, and he saw a deck of cards in his pocket — the very cards they had been playing poker with the night before.

Mort fell to his knees and clasped his hands over his face as gut-wrenching sobs overtook him. "Nooooo!"

His tear-filled hands were shaking when Captain Hawk walked over.

Hawk looked sternly at Brooklyn. "Close that poncho!" He had to put a kibosh on this. "No one should be opening the ponchos!"

Captain Hawk turned toward the rest of the men who were picking up the bodies. "DO YOU UNDERSTAND ME?"

Hawk called for men from the second platoon to come over and carry the body of Sanchez. He signaled for Mort and Brooklyn to walk behind Deadeye and Chief.

"Come on." Brooklyn nudged Mort.

Mort didn't move. Amos, being one of Mort's closest buddies, went over to Mort.

"It can't be." Mort felt sick. He was so dizzy he didn't know if he could stand up.

"Come on. We have to get moving." Amos grabbed Mort by the arm. Mort came along.

"It was Sanchez... he's dead."

"I know. We're gonna make it."

"Ya. Make it to our graves."

Mort stumbled along, silently staring ahead. Somehow his feet were moving, but he felt more like he was floating outside his body. He was totally disconnected from his surroundings. He was dimly aware he was in the middle of a war. He couldn't stop the thoughts racing randomly through his mind. Thoughts of Sanchez. Laughing. Cards. Gunshots. The bullet hole in his head. "We played cards last night. I can still see the look he gave me at the helipad. I should have known."

Amos listened, but remained silent. Mort turned to stare at Amos. Amos would help him get to wherever they were going. Good old Amos. They had made it this far... maybe they would make it out of here together.

Fabe and Mex were carrying one end of the poncho that held Cal. Two other men from the third platoon carried the other end. Rigamortis hadn't set in yet, making it difficult to carry the slumped body. They had to hold the poncho high or it dragged on the ground in the middle.

The men walked along in silence. Everyone had the same thought — they could be next. No one said it out loud.

Fabe thought of the day before when they were on LZ Professional. Cal was happy because he had received a letter from his wife, and she had sent him chewing gum. Fabe had traded some of his cookies for some gum. "War is hell," he said to no one in particular.

Brian heard him, but there was no more to say. He fell in line behind Fabe, carrying Cal's rucksack and gun. He didn't complain that his load had doubled. He was thankful to be alive. The least he could do was keep Cal's rucksack with him so any personal items he carried could be sent back home to his wife.

Since Lil' Bro had the radio, he didn't carry any of the wounded. He followed close behind Merdis, who was helping to carry CJ in an upright position.

Clark followed behind Merdis pushing the prisoner along. If it were up to him, he'd shoot the bastard. But he would follow the Captain's orders and see that he was unharmed.

Second Platoon led the way to a clearing, only a quarter of a klick ahead. They stopped when they came to a bomb crater large enough that part of the company could spend the night there. They would be packed close together, but the shallow crater would afford them cover for some of the men and the wounded. Darkness had closed in, making it impossible to dig foxholes.

Before organizing the men for the night, Captain Hawk radioed into TOC to request a dustoff. He knew they didn't like to fly after dark, but they were in desperate need to get the wounded out. He also wanted to send the prisoner out. When he received a report that there was only one chopper available, he shook his head in disgust. It meant they could only send out those who had the most serious wounds.

Brian and Fabe helped Ferg to the area the medics designated. They put him down next to Harris. Ferg could see

Harris was groggy from the morphine, but he was anxious to report on CJ. "Ferg! I saw CJ! I seen 'em carryin' him. He's alive."

"Praise the Lord!"

"He's not lookin' good, but Captain's called for a dustoff. He'll be getting' help soon... so will we."

"The morphine's wearin' off. I'm prayin' we're gonna get outta here. I ain't sure I can hold on till mornin'. I'm not that strong."

"Get those most critical ready! I hear a chopper! We'll have to..." Captain Hawk's words were cut off by the sound of heavy gunfire. "Those bastards!"

The sound of the chopper blades faded away. Voices came over the radio to update Captain Hawk. The chopper would not come in tonight. They had to abort the mission due to the heavy gunfire from the NVA. He was informed that Colonel Stinson, the Battalion Commander, was killed that afternoon in enemy fire while attempting to extract wounded from Alpha Company. The 1/52 had lost its commander.

Captain Hawk gave orders to the platoon leaders for setting up the night lager. "First platoon and those in mortars with rifles will watch the north side of the crater. Stay inside the crater so you have some cover. Set up the mortar tube behind the men with the rifles. Headquarters will be inside the crater on the south-east side. Second platoon will be outside the crater, covering Headquarters. The wounded and dead will be on the south-west side of the crater with the third platoon outside the crater covering them. The perimeter will be jagged. That's okay. Just be sure the men are spread out to cover all sides."

Next, he called for air support. Hopefully, they would send a Spooky to pound the area tonight. Ideally, they would wipe out the NVA in the area. More realistically, they would give some light from the illumination flares so they could see the NVA when they were in stealth mode during the night and keep them at bay.

Merdis, Doc Bauer, and the other medics would take turns sitting with CJ throughout the night. Merdis sat at the edge of the crater, leaning against the crater wall. He supported CJ in a sitting position while the medics checked on the other wounded men. His rhythmic, tortured breaths were all Merdis heard. He was oblivious to the groaning and cries of the other wounded around him.

Harris and Ferg laid side by side only a few feet from CJ. "Ah ain't never hurt like dis."

Harris could hear Ferg moaning whenever his morphine was wearing off. He knew Ferg's wounds were more severe than his own. "Hang on. They'll git us out in the mornin'. We're goin' home. Just keep thinkin' about that."

Harris reflected on the conversation between CJ and Ferg from that morning. It seemed funny at the time. *What a stupid thought to write a war comedy. There is nothing funny about war. Nothing at all.*

By 2200 hours the men of Charlie Company were settled in their night position. The second and third platoon sat outside the crater. Scrub brush and an occasional small tree were the only cover they had. The third platoon looked out over a rice paddy in the distance, while the second platoon saw only part of the rice paddy. The rest of the area was covered in scrub providing a perfect place for the NVA to creep up on them. The rest of the men on watch were lying flat on their bellies in the crater facing toward the jungle, rifles ready for the attack each man feared.

Twenty minutes later the Spooky circled above, lighting up the sky and surrounding areas.

Brian sat to Fabe's left, with Lil' Bro to Fabe's right. Their rucksacks were at their sides. They did not need to take turns keeping watch tonight. No one would sleep. The NVA was out there, and every man anticipated an attack at any minute.

Fabe wanted to reach into his rucksack to grab a can of C-rations. "I'm so hungry I could eat ham and muthas." Unwilling to put his rifle down, for even a minute, he'd have to go hungry tonight. A cigarette would sure help calm his nerves. "I'd give anything for a cigarette." The glow from a cigarette would be like a bullseye on a target for the NVA.

"I'd give anything for a foxhole." Brian knew he'd have to stay sitting up tonight and be on high alert. It would be a miracle if they didn't get attacked.

Lil' Bro remained silent. He thoughts were not of cigarettes or foxholes. They were of his wife. Would he ever see her again? Would he see his son? It all seemed so impossible right now.

As Lil' Bro sat there expecting to be assaulted at any moment, his thoughts went back to the events of the day. He shuddered. He had seen war movies, but this was nothing like those movies. Seeing men dying was nothing like he had imagined. There was no way to describe the horror he felt while listening to the wounded men moaning, knowing there was no help in sight. Fear consumed him, making it hard to be rational. He agonized over the thought of shooting someone.

Lil' Bro felt glad that he was positioned next to Fabe. Thank God for giving him someone to lean on. "I don't know if I can shoot someone... What do you feel when you shoot someone?"

"A slight recoil."

"That's not funny. Really, Fabe! I need to know."

"Well, first of all, if they're shooting at you, you rarely get close enough to see 'em. You only see the muzzle flash. You can't think of gooks as real people... just the enemy. And if that ain't enough to convince you to kill the dinks, think about Sanchez and Cal. Kill them or they'll kill you."

"I guess."

"You're trained for the infantry. What'd they teach ya? How to shoot a rifle."

"But that was different."

"You better think about it. We practiced at targets of men. They tested us and made sure we could shoot accurately. They trained us to be killers. That's just a fact."

Lil' Bro was quiet. Fabe was right. Since he'd been in the field so much had happened. Everything was a blur. It all seemed like a nightmare. He tried to sort out things in his mind. "When they called for a dustoff, they said the crew had to turn around due to heavy gunfire. I thought they didn't shoot at a Medivac chopper?"

Fabe took a deep breath. He hated to give discouraging information to Lil' Bro, but he might as well tell him the truth. "They're not supposed to shoot at a chopper with a red cross because it's not armed. Sometimes the bastards shoot at the Medivacs and don't give a shit. There are obviously no Medivacs in flying condition. The gooks shot 'em. They either crashed or were too damaged to go out. You saw the downed chopper in the rice paddy when we were dropped in. They shot down that Medivac. There were probably wounded men in it, along with the medics. If you think about that you won't have a problem shooting those shit-faced dinks."

Lil' Bro was quiet for several minutes thinking about what Fabe said. The sky lit up in streaks of red. It made him think of hell. Every few minutes the roar stopped, only to return from another direction. "Are we going to have to listen to the gunship all night?"

"I hope so." Fabe answered without taking his eyes off the area beyond their perimeter. "When night comes, the NVA come out. They have tunnels everywhere and you don't know when or where they'll appear. Without Puff the Magic Dragon, we'd be in big trouble."

"Puff the Magic Dragon?"

Fabe was glad Lil' Bro was asking questions. It helped take his mind off of Sanchez and Cal. "Ya, that's what they call the Spooky. The stream of the tracers look like a dragon's breath." He watched the bright red tracer rounds shoot to the ground lighting up the blackness.

"They probably won't keep it up too long. Alpha and Bravo are out here somewhere, so they're limited where they can shoot."

"I don't see how anyone can survive out there."

"They can't survive if they are out there in the path of the gunship. But they can survive if they are in their tunnels."

"Lay it on me, Fabe. We're not going to get outta here, are we?"

"Don't go ape on me. You gotta hang tough. Concentrate on survival right now. Don't dwell on tomorrow. We'll make it." Fabe was afraid there would be more wounded and killed before they got out of this one, but he didn't say so to Lil' Bro.

Fabe stared into the night. He wiped his damp face on his shirt, but it stunk of blood and rice paddy, only making the situation worse. His back ached, his legs were getting numb, and his palms were sweaty. His clothes were covered with Cal's blood and smelled like rusting metal. He swiped his tongue across his dry lips. Some of that gum from Cal would sure be good now. He took a swig from his canteen. He had used some of the precious water to wash the blood from his hands earlier. He hoped they would be resupplying them with water soon. The long, low moans from the wounded ground on his nerves. Death hung in the air like weights suspended on a string.

"That moaning gives me the heebie-jeebies." Brian whispered.

"I hope they can get a huey in tomorrow." Fabe thought the worst thing that could happen to someone was to be wounded and slowly die because they couldn't get a chopper in.

"I hope we're still *alive* tomorrow to get the men on the huey." Brian closed his eyes and prayed they would live to see daylight.

Fabe continued staring into the darkness, reflecting on the sight of the men mutilated by the ambush. He had seen a helluva lot, but watching your friends die and hearing them moaning in pain with no help in sight was torture.

Amos, Cooper, Brooklyn, JR, Mort, Dan, Rico and the rest of the mortar platoon were lying close to the bodies wrapped in ponchos. They couldn't move because of the number of men crammed into the crater. Their muscles ached from lying in one position so long. The moans of the wounded continued relentlessly. They could hear someone from the first platoon crying softly. Everyone's clothes were getting stiff from the mud and blood, and smelled of stagnant water from the rice paddy.

Mort was still having trouble thinking straight. The sight of Sanchez in the poncho haunted him. He kept hearing his laugh as he was winning at cards last night. A passage from Macbeth popped into his mind:

"To-morrow, and to-morrow, and to-morrow,
Creeps in this petty pace from day to day,
To the last syllable of recorded time;
And all our yesterdays have lighted fools
The way to dusty death. Out, out brief candle!
Life's but a walking shadow, a poor player
That struts and frets his hour upon the stage,
And then is heard no more. It is a tale
Told by an idiot, full of sound and fury,
Signifying nothing."

Mort looked at Amos. Thank God Amos was there. He had guided him through the last couple of hours. Without Amos, he didn't think he would have made it.

Dan was next to Rico. They were positioned near the wounded men. The metallic smell of dried blood permeated the air around them. The sounds made him shudder. Sobbing mingled with another man's whimper. Moaning and men calling out desperate for some relief, "God, please, just let me die!"

Dan shuddered. "I don't know how long I can lay here and listen to that. It's gettin' on my last nerve." A muscle twitched involuntarily at the corner of his eye.

"Get a grip!" Rico was having problems staying still, but he had to keep calm. It could be the difference between walking away and a shallow grave. "I don't know about you, but I wanna get out of here alive. If you panic, you won't make it. I have a wife and two kids to think about."

"Well, I'll be. I didn't know y'all had a family."

"Oh, sure. My wife has raven black hair. Real pretty gal. My daughter is three, and my little boy is two. I joined the Army because I couldn't find a job in Puerto Rico."

"Y'all got a good reason to get outta here."

"You bet I do!"

Earlier, around dusk, Brooklyn had seen a figure peeking out of the jungle from behind a tree. He disappeared before anyone could get a shot off. Now Brooklyn was lying on his stomach, staying low to the ground, feeling surrounded. It had been quiet since the gunship had made its last pass an hour ago. A haze smelling of gunpowder and burned earth had settled over the night. Fires were smoldering in the distance to his right. He saw movement by the fires — or were his eyes playing tricks on him? He expected the NVA to attack at any moment.

Cooper lay next to Brooklyn staring into the darkness outside the perimeter. "What if I see something move?"

"Open up."

"What if I can't see what it is? It might not be the enemy."

"Poinsonally, I doan give a shit. Yuh wanna end up like Sanchez?"

Brooklyn had a good point. Cooper ran his fingers through his dirty hair. He thought about Brooklyn's comment earlier. "Would you really kill the prisoner?"

"Damn right! The doity mutha fucka deserves it."

Cooper was having trouble processing everything. "Are you crazy? He's just a kid."

"A kid who tried tuh kill us guys. He'll be sent tuh the rear where he'll have plenty'a food and watta. He'll be warm and dry and safe."

Cooper was silent.

"And us guys are stuck here. Wet, tired, hungry, an' gettin' shot at. Carryin' around our friends that're dead. Listenin' tuh the moanin'. That might be you tomorrow night. Think about that."

CHAPTER 6

Carrying the Casualties

4 March 1969 – 0430 Hours

Merdis and the medics took turns sitting with CJ during the night. He was slipping in and out of consciousness. Blood was seeping through the bandage around his chest, soaking Merdis' shirt. "Doc! Doc! Git over here!"

Doc Bauer was crawling inside the circle of men, checking on the wounded. All he could do for them right now was give them morphine for their pain and try to control the bleeding. He crawled over to Merdis and CJ. "What?"

"A minute ago his breathin' was loud and raspy – kinda gurgling. Then he stopped breathin' for a minute. Now he's raspy. He feels really cold."

Doc sat in silence as he listened to CJ. He had heard this before. "It's the death rattle. Hold him close so he doesn't feel alone. There's no more we can do."

Merdis tightened his grip on CJ, hugging him close. CJ let out a long breath. It was his last.

"He's gone. You can lay him down now."

Merdis continued to hold CJ, tears trickling down his cheek. He felt as if he was in a nightmare, totally disconnected from the men around him. He felt both grief and relief. When Hawk called in to TOC, he didn't even hear him.

It was an hour and a half until dawn. Hawk called in to request gunships for 0630 hours to cover their initial movement of the morning.

Right on schedule, two gunships pounded the area surrounding the men of Charlie Company. Hawk called for an urgent dustoff and resupply of ammo before they pulled out. Hopefully, the effects of the Spooky during the night and the gunships this morning had made the area secure enough for a chopper to come in. Clenching his teeth, he watched a helicopter approach. As it drew near, his shoulders sagged when he heard the percussive sound of sniper fire. Again, the rescue mission was aborted.

Each man checked his supplies, as ordered by Hawk. The first and second platoon were already low on ammunition. Deadeye and Chief had used half of their HEAT explosives.

The platoon leaders made sure the ammo was distributed equally.

Fabe and Lil' Bro checked their ammunition. Fabe had already eaten two cans of rations this morning. "You better eat something when you have the chance."

Lil' Bro pulled out a can labeled, "Ham and eggs, chopped." That should make a good breakfast. Taking out his P38, he opened the can, and was ready to dig in. The greyish color of the mush in the can turned his stomach. Cal's grey face was the same color as the mush in the can. He could taste the bile in his throat. Swallowing hard, he took a deep breath. He threw down the can and walked away.

Fabe was watching Lil' Bro. There was nothing he could do to help him. Some things you just had to deal with on your own.

By 0710 hours Charlie Company was ready to move on. They were down to ninety-four able men. Today's priority was finding a place a chopper could get in.

The third platoon was assigned to carry the dead and wounded, as well as guard the prisoner. The bodies were easier to carry now that rigamortis had set in. Fabe and Mex went to help Ferg hobble onto one leg. Ferg placed an arm around each of them. He gritted his teeth, but didn't complain. "Is CJ ok?"

Fabe and Mex looked at each other but didn't answer.

"Don't pull dat silent shit with me! Ah wanna know how CJ is! He dead or alive?"

"Dead."

Ferg let out a moan. "It shoulda been me, ya know. It was mah turn to walk point... Ah never should have let 'im take it for me. Can't nobody say it weren't my fault."

Since they did not have the time or resources to make a litter, Brian would have to carry Harris. The severity of the wounds to his shoulder and leg left him unable to walk, even with assistance.

Brian lifted Harris so he could balance on his left leg. When he stood up, he only came up to Brian's shoulders. Brian grabbed Harris by his left wrist and raised his arm over his head. He then squatted down on his knee. Putting his left hand between Harris' legs, he grasped his left leg. Then he hefted Harris over his shoulders. He brought his arm around Harris' thigh and shifted his weight over his shoulders. Then he slowly stood up, carrying Harris using the fireman's carry. Harris hooked his left arm under Brian's right arm so Brian would have one arm free to carry his M60.

The Second Platoon led the way. They hadn't gone far when they received enemy fire. Everyone hit the ground. Ferg let out a cry of anguish when he landed on the ground with a thump. He grabbed at his wounded leg and gritted his teeth as the pain shot through his entire body. Fabe and Mex paid no attention to him as they raised their weapons ready to fire. Keeping alive was the priority.

There was an exchange of rifle fire for a few minutes. Then silence.

"2-3 to Alpha 6!"

"Go ahead 2-3."

"Sniper. I think we took him out. Point man hit."

"Roger. On our way."

Captain Hawk and his RTO made their way to the front. A few minutes later they were ready to get on their way again.

"Alpha 6 to 3-2."

Merdis grabbed the handset from Lil' Bro. "Go ahead Alpha 6."

"One wounded. Shot in left side. Can't walk. When you come through have your men pick him up."

"Yes, Sir!"

By 1320 hours they had only gone a kilometer. Every time they made a little headway, they encountered enemy fire. They were now carrying five bodies and three wounded. The other three wounded men were able to walk with assistance. A third of the men were taken out of combat to transport these men.

When they came to a small clearing, Captain Hawk signaled the men to halt. They sat down to take a break and chow down. The men who were carrying the wounded and dead, and those carrying two rucksacks needed the rest.

By now Lil' Bro was feeling the gnawing pain of hunger. He took out his P38 and opened cans of turkey and peaches. He gobbled them down without even tasting what he was eating. He started gulping water from his canteen.

Mort sat down by Amos and opened a can of C-rations. His attention turned to the men around him. They looked so different than when he had studied each person yesterday on the helipad. Glancing at the line of poncho-wrapped bodies, he remembered the way Cal's eyes met his yesterday, as if he knew he wouldn't make it. He counted five bodies — last night there were only four.

He looked at Doc Bauer, who was tending a wounded man a few feet away. "Who died?"

Doc never looked up from his patient. "CJ."

Mort bowed his head and spoke softly to Amos, "It would have been me. If I hadn't been transferred to mortars, I probably would have been walking point."

Amos took the picture from inside his helmet and stared

at it for a moment. Only one more month and he would see Judy. Grabbing his paper from his rucksack, he added a few lines to his letter.

One month from today I will be heading home. Yesterday was awful. While we were being dropped into our location, a sniper was shooting at us. We landed in a rice paddy. My feet are still wet and my clothes full of mud. We started out to find our night lager when all hell broke loose. The first platoon lost several men – I don't know how many, but the loss is significant. We are on a hill that is overrun with NVA. I am lucky to be in the mortar platoon so I don't have to walk point. We are more protected than the other squads. We are on a short break, but we will be on the move soon.

Cooper put down his load and ate two cans of c-rations. His stomach begged for more food, but that was it for now. He had to rest for a few minutes. His body felt as if it were made of lead. His clothes were still wet in some places. Where they had dried, they were stiff from the mud. He ran his fingers through his hair. He could feel mud caked in his hair from the rice paddy. Cooper looked at Brooklyn, who was sitting next to him. "How long have you been in Nam?"

"Since June. Only three months tuh go."

"How'd you last this long? I don't think I'll make it."

Brooklyn managed a smile for Cooper. "Yuh'll make it. All the missions aren't like this. This is one of the wawhst I've been on."

"How are we gonna get outta here? We can't even get the wounded out." Cooper again ran his fingers through his filthy hair.

"Yuh can't think like that. If yuh do, yuh'll nevah make it. Take one day at a time… no, take one hour at a time."

Brooklyn pulled out a can of rations. "Yuh got a goil back home?"

"Kinda. She's more of a friend, but I've already gotten three letters from her, and a picture. I'd show you, but I don't have the energy to get out my wallet. I never knew a letter could mean so much."

"I appreciate a lot of things I used tuh take fawh granted, okay? Mail. Hamburgers. A soft bed. Cold watta."

Since the clearing wasn't large enough to call for a chopper, Captain Hawk decided to approach the prisoner while the men were taking a break. He took the bag off the prisoner's head and gave him a drink of water. It was vital to get him to the rear for interrogation. He decided to question him again. After being tied up and pushed along he might be more willing to talk.

Hawk threatened to turn him over to the men. After a long exchange with the prisoner in Vietnamese, Captain Hawk had information to send back to TOC. The prisoner was working with a division protecting NVA regimental headquarters. At least two battalions were involved. He was sure the prisoner knew more, and there were probably at least double the amount of NVA involved. When the prisoner got to TOC, they would try to get more information on the location of the NVA headquarters.

Hawk wondered if the attack on the Special Forces Camp was a diversion. According to the prisoner, they had landed on the fringe of the operation. Making progress was nearly impossible. It was so difficult to know where the NVA were. They built fortresses underground connected with tunnels. TOC was putting pressure on Charlie Company to move faster. Right now he had to concentrate on finding a secure area to get the wounded out and dig in for the night.

Before heading out again, Hawk met with the platoon leaders. "We'll circle toward the west, and head back toward the area we were in last night. Hopefully, we'll find a suitable place for a dustoff. If we don't find one, we'll try to secure the area we were in last night. I haven't seen anything better."

Hawk knew TOC would be unhappy if they returned to

last night's area instead of moving forward. His men came first, and priority was getting the wounded out.

They took off with the Second Platoon in the lead. At 1410 hours the point man came to a dead stop.

"2-3 to Alpha 6."

"Go ahead 2-3."

"Possible tunnel."

"Roger. On our way. Have your men check it out and get your tunnel rat ready."

This time Fabe and Mex carefully eased Ferg to the ground, then helped Brian ease Harris down. Ferg was getting extremely tired and leaned on them heavily. It would be a few minutes before Captain Hawk worked his way to the front of the line and gave orders on how to proceed. They took advantage of this time to give Ferg and Harris some water and let them rest.

The heat of the day was so intense it became the enemy. Fabe felt his energy draining fast. The sweat ran and heat enveloped every part of his body. He wiped the sweat with his C scarf. Occasionally, a small cloud appeared in the sky — even a few minutes of relief from the sun made a difference. Fabe drained his second canteen, which only had enough water in it to wet his parched lips. Pulling out his third canteen, he chugged down half of its contents. His thoughts went to his home in Wisconsin, where the temperature rarely was above the nineties and there was always plenty of cool water. Maybe the guys who were wounded were the lucky ones. They would be getting out of this hellhole. That is, if they ever got a chopper in.

Fabe's muddy, bloody clothes smelled like a slaughterhouse. He longed to remove his boots and let his feet dry out. He looked at Lil' Bro. He looked pale and was staring into the distance. His face was beaded with sweat.

Fabe walked over to Lil' Bro. "Put your pack and radio

down for a minute and drink some water. Sit down and take your helmet off until we get going."

Lil' Bro nodded and did as he was told, guzzling the warm canteen water. Fabe could see he was getting very hot, but he wasn't too worried about heat stroke as long as Lil' Bro was still sweating.

"Pour a little water over your face to help cool you down."

"I don't want to use up my water — what if we run out?"

"Supply choppers will be dropping water jugs, along with food and ammo — usually every three days. They re-supply everything."

A muffled explosion startled Lil' Bro. He grabbed his gun and fell flat on the ground.

Fabe chuckled. "They threw a hand grenade in the tunnel. You could tell by the muffled sound. They'll probably send someone down in the tunnel to see if there's anything or anyone left there, so you can stay sitting for a while."

Fabe took his pocket calendar out of his wallet and put an X on March fourth. He reached for a cigarette and lit it with his Zippo lighter. The back of the lighter was engraved, *WHEN I DIE I'M SURE TO GO TO HEAVEN, BECAUSE I'VE SPENT MY TIME IN HELL.*

He took a drag from his cigarette, staring at the bodies wrapped in ponchos. Ponchos were well used in Vietnam. During the monsoon season they served as a raincoat during the day, and a cover to keep the rain off at night. Sometimes they huddled under the poncho to cover the light of a cigarette in the night. When they were on a less dangerous mission, they would use them to make tents for shade during the hottest part of the day. Just like he used to do at home. He remembered his mother helping him and the neighbor boy, Wayne. She would string a rope between two trees and put a blanket over the rope to make a tent. They would make believe it was a teepee and play

Cowboys and Indians. Or sometimes she would put it on the trees by the road. Then he and Wayne would set up a Kool-Aid stand using the tent as their store. He wondered what Wayne was doing now. He had been in a motorcycle accident right after high school graduation and messed up his foot pretty bad. He'd never pass the physical if he did get his draft notice. He would remain in the 'world'. A world that seemed like only a vague memory today.

After 15 minutes, the radio jolted Fabe from his reverie as he heard the report that four NVA had been killed. It was time to get moving again.

They had been walking for twenty minutes when Merdis grabbed the radio handset from Lil' Bro.

"3-2 to Alpha 6."

"Go ahead 3-2."

"Y'all need to stop for a few minutes. One of the wounded died."

"Copy that. We'll stop for five. Alpha 6 out."

Five minutes later they were humping again. Sweat dripped off Fabe's nose. A sticky wet feeling covered literally every pore on his body. Exhaustion was taking its toll – he didn't think he could take another step. Somehow his feet kept moving, supporting Ferg and keeping pace with Mex.

His mouth was parched. He bent down and picked up two smooth stones and handed one to Lil' Bro. "Suck on the stone. It helps. At least you'll get some spit in your mouth."

Brian picked up Harris, wondering how long he could carry him. Then he remembered a Bible passage from Isiah: "*If you pour yourself out for the hungry and satisfy the desire of the afflicted, then shall your light rise in the darkness and your gloom be as the noonday. And the Lord will guide you continually and satisfy your desire in scorched places and make your bones strong; and you shall be like a watered garden, like a spring of water, whose waters do not fail.*" Knowing the Lord would help him, Brian felt his steps lightening even as he walked in the sweltering heat carrying his burden.

At 1530 hours they heard rifle fire from the front of the line. Everyone hit the ground. Fabe and Mex tried to let Ferg down gently.

"2-3 to Alpha 6."

"Go ahead 2-3."

"One killed when coming outta tunnel. Wearing green uniform."

"Roger. On my way."

Captain Hawk made it to the front of the line where the point man and the rest of the second platoon were on the ground with their rifles pointing at the tunnel entrance where the dead NVA soldier laid.

Hawk decided it was too dangerous to send in a tunnel rat, so he ordered them to detonate several hand grenades and throw them into the tunnel.

Near the entrance to the tunnel was a small clearing large enough for a chopper to land. Captain Hawk called for a resupply ship to bring in ammo, water, and medical supplies and pick up the wounded. The first and second platoons quickly cleared any brush that might hinder the helicopter's approach, while the mortar platoon kept guard on the perimeter.

At 1545 hours everyone was relieved to hear the rhythmic thwop-thwop of the helicopter blades. Tears formed in Harris's eyes as he heard the chopper come closer. "Please, Lord, let me get on da chopper dis time."

Men from the second and third platoon ran to the wounded and prepared to take them to the chopper. They knew the resupply ship would not touch down, so they had to be ready to hoist the wounded up. They would load the six wounded men and the prisoner. The dead would have to wait until they could get the next chopper in.

The crew of the airship began shoving crates of supplies off as they began descending, then hovered at three feet off the ground. Chief and Brian picked up Harris. He didn't mind the extra pain caused by the men running with him. For the first time, he felt as if he might make it.

Brian and Chief were hoisting Harris up to hand him off to the gunner inside. Gunshots ripped through the air as snipers opened fire. The door gunner fell backward. The chopper took a dip before lifting off as the pilot took a bullet in his left hand. Chief and Brian dropped to the ground. Harris let out a moan as he thumped to the ground. They laid flat as the bullets flew over them.

Ferg let out a yelp when Fabe and Mex dropped to the ground. "Those muhfuckas!"

Some of the others were not so lucky. One man from the second platoon that was right behind them was hit. They dropped the wounded man they were carrying as they screamed out in agony.

"Man hit! MEDIC!"

Brooklyn and JR crawled to the injured men to get them out of the line of fire. Doc Bauer and another medic ran to tend their wounds. Without waiting for direction from Captain Hawk, one of the men grabbed his M79 grenade launcher and pointed it in the direction of the sniper fire. As soon as the grenade hit the ground the shooting stopped. He had either hit his target or made the sniper withdraw.

After the gunfire stopped, Brooklyn and Cooper were among the men who ran out and grabbed the supplies that were thrown off the resupply ship. Brooklyn grabbed a case of ammo. Only one five-gallon jug of water had been dropped off, and Captain Hawk gave it to the medic to disperse among the wounded.

Doc Bauer was tending the two that had been hit with sniper fire. "Couldn't the door gunner drop some supplies for us?"

Chief ditched his 45 handgun and grabbed an M16 with

an ammo belt from one of the wounded. It would be a lot more to carry with the Recoilless, but well worth it for the power it had.

"Let's get the hell out of here!" Hawk barked.

Again, the second platoon took the lead. Next was mortars, followed by the third platoon, now carrying six bodies and the wounded who were unable to walk. Others were assisting the other wounded men, as needed. The first platoon was bringing up the rear and guarding the prisoner.

CHAPTER 7

Back to the Crater

1630 Hours

The men made it back to the area of the bomb crater where they had spent the previous night. To Lil' Bro it seemed more like a week ago than a day ago. Had they only been here one day? It felt like an eternity. Now he understood why the guys referred to anything outside Vietnam as "the world". That was the real world. He was in some part of hell – totally detached from any kind of civilization.

Hawk met with the platoon and squad leaders. "We'll set up for the night near the same crater as last night. We'll stay a little farther from the jungle. Since the choppers took so much fire this morning, we gotta clear a much larger area for them. We have to get the wounded guys outta here."

"First and second platoon: Divide your squads – half of your men will clear the area south of the crater. Be sure it's big enough. We need to provide a helluva lot more clearing or we'll have a repeat of last night. Post guards to provide cover for those clearing the area. The other half start digging fox holes on the south side of the crater."

"Third platoon and mortars: Mortars set up the tube in the center of the perimeter. Half of the platoon start digging foxholes for yourselves and headquarters. The other half clear the brush outside the perimeter to increase our night vision."

"Third platoon start digging foxholes on the north side of the crater. Set up trip wires and claymores outside the perimeter – that side will be the easiest for the NVA to sneak up."

Captain Hawk turned his attention to Clark. "Turner – have your men keep a close eye on the prisoner."

"Yes, Sir."

"When the choppers come in, mortars will provide security for them. First and second platoons provide security around the perimeter."

"Merdis, the third platoon will load the wounded. Assign men so they know exactly who they are loading – who will lift the wounded, who will load their rucksacks, and who will load the prisoner."

"Shake a leg!"

An hour later, the area was nearly ready for the chopper. As sniper fire erupted, everyone hit the ground. All the men laid heavy fire into the area of the sniper. The sniper was either hit or retreated, but not before he had reached his target, wounding two men from the second Platoon.

Captain Hawk called TOC and requested an urgent dustoff with a gunship to provide protection. He also requested they bring in food, water, ammo, and medical supplies.

Forty-five minutes later two gunships appeared and pounded the surrounding area for thirty minutes. The men of Charlie Company welcomed the sound of the two– and three-quarter-inch rockets spewed out by the gunship. The door gunner's machine gun scattered bullets at the rate of 4,000 rounds per minute. Combined with the thump-thump-thump of the helicopter blades, it was a symphony to the men on the ground.

Less than ten minutes after the gunships left, they heard the next choppers coming in the distance. The men of the third platoon ran to pick up the most severely wounded. They carried them to the outside of the area cleared for the chopper. The men from the mortar platoon went with them, rifles ready.

The first and second platoon scattered around the perimeter of the crater.

A gunship and a resupply chopper appeared on the horizon. They hovered in the center of the crater and threw out a crate of ammunition.

"Get your ass lower!" Fabe yelled at the pilot.

The pilot held the bird steady six feet off the ground. The gunner pushed another box of ammo off the chopper.

Brooklyn pointed his rifle at the pilot. "Yuh fuckin' coward! Get that choppuh down here, or I'll shoot your asses down! Yuh'll see what it's like tuh be stuck here."

The chopper pilot responded, descending to four feet off the ground as enemy fire broke out. The gunship pounded shells into the direction the fire came from, along with the first and second platoon.

They managed to get all the wounded loaded, including Ferg and Harris. They also shoved the prisoner on the chopper. The choppers took off leaving behind the three walking wounded and the six bodies.

Fabe, Brian, and Mex were assigned to one fox hole. Lil' Bro was in the fox hole to their right with Merdis. Fabe and Brian grabbed their entrenching tools and resumed digging as soon as the choppers lifted off.

Fabe ignored the sweat running in his eyes. "I'm sure as hell gonna dig deep tonight."

"I don't think I'll ever complain about diggin' a fox hole again. Last night was enough for me. It gives me the heebie-jeebies just thinking about it." Brian's size gave him an advantage in throwing the dirt out of the hole as they dug deeper.

"Maybe we can get a couple hours of sleep tonight."

"Hey, Bro! Are we having fun yet?"

Lil' Bro looked up from the hole he was digging and managed a crooked smile. "Fuck you, Fabe!"

Fabe laughed.

After their hole was dug to their satisfaction, Fabe got out clacker wire and set up claymore mines a little distance out from their foxholes. They were wired to a remote control which was placed on the edge of the foxhole for easy access. When detonated, the claymore fired an arrangement of 700 steel balls like a shotgun in a sixty-degree arc for 100 meters.

Beyond the claymores Brian and Mex set up trip flares. It provided some protection from anyone trying to sneak up on them during the night. If a flare was detonated it would give off a bright light lasting a minute and a half.

By 2000 hours the men were settled in their foxholes eating more c-rations. They had to eat everything cold, as it was too risky to start any kind of fire. Fabe was finishing his fourth canteen of water. Tomorrow they should be dropping a new supply. As usual, they had packed enough C-rations and water to last three days. Tomorrow would be day three.

"Why the hell didn't they drop water and rations while they were here?"

"Beats me. I'm sure they'll be back in the mornin' to pick up the rest of the wounded and the dead guys. They'll bring it then." Brian was always thinking on the positive side. Sometimes that irritated Fabe.

"Geez Louise. They managed two drops of ammo. You'd think they could bring water. I'm down to my last canteen."

Brian drained a canteen and put it in his rucksack. "Me, too. Good thing we didn't have time to eat the first day or we'd be out of food, too."

Chief was sitting in the foxhole next to Deadeye and Dan. His eyes fell on the rifle he had exchanged for his handgun. "I always thought it would be so cool to carry a rifle and be in a war. When I was a kid, I played war with my brothers all the time."

Dan stared out into nowhere. "I think it was my eighth birthday when I got an army set. It came with a helmet, hand grenade, rifle, and a small canteen. Everything was plastic but it seemed real enough to me."

Chief nodded. "My brothers were older, and always had better stuff than I did. So, I did all kinds of odd jobs to save up enough money to buy a toy automatic rifle from the Ben Franklin store. It was bigger and better than anything my brothers had. I felt tough. We'd shoot at each other and run around like we were in battle."

Dan nodded in agreement. "Did you watch *Combat!* on TV?"

"Sure did. I was really excited when it went from black and white to color."

"The sergeant's name was Saunders. We tried to imitate everything he did." Deadeye smiled at his childhood memories. "I played war with the neighbor boy. We hid behind trees and crawled around on the ground. We'd try to imitate the sound of gunfire when we shot at each other. Then one of us would fall down pretending we were dead."

Chief became serious. "Then my mother would call us in for cookies and milk. We had no idea what war really was." He turned his head toward the ponchos lined up just a few feet away. "No idea."

Brian, Fabe, and Mex took turns sleeping. Mex volunteered to take the first watch. Although there wasn't room to lay down in the fox hole, it only took minutes for Fabe and Brian to doze off.

Mex stared into the night with only his head peeking out of the foxhole. He placed two hand grenades in front of him. He had his rifle ready to fire in an instant. It was much quieter than last night. No men moaning, and no Spookys lighting up the sky. In the distance there were traces of fire where Puff the Magic Dragon was providing support to Alpha Company. As Mex scrutinized the landscape, he could imagine the NVA creeping in. There was no real movement he could detect. He looked up at the stars. It took him back. Only four months ago he was sitting outside under the stars at home. He thought about the night before he left for Vietnam. His wife had clung to him knowing it was their last night together for a long time. She had looked so beautiful with the moonlight reflecting off her long blonde hair. Would he ever get back to the world, or would she soon be a widow? Mex knew he had to focus and stay alert. He couldn't get distracted. His life depended on it, and he sure as hell was going to try to stay alive so he and his wife could build a future together.

At 0100 hours Mex woke Fabe for his turn to take watch. Fabe became instantly alert. The air was cool. It was a relief from the heat of the day. There was only a sliver of a moon – it made the night feel falsely calm. As he studied his surroundings, everything took on an unfamiliar slant. The bushes almost looked as if they were moving. Was there some movement behind the distant tree? Fabe was careful not to let his imagination grow wild. If he didn't divert his thoughts he would not be able to control them. Once you got spooked it was hard to think rationally.

He directed his thoughts to home. March in Wisconsin was bitterly cold. His old man would be busy plowing snow. Snow. He was dying of heat, and his old man was freezing. Well, not really. The house would be warm and cozy, and his mother would have the cookstove going. Their stove was a combination of gas and wood. There's nothing like warming yourself next to a wood stove when you come in from below zero conditions… and his mother's cooking! She cooked up some great meals on that stove. Some of her food would sure be good now. Beef soup. Fried chicken. Homemade mac 'n cheese. Raw-fried potatoes and steak. Fabe's mouth was watering. He swallowed hard. Now he was miserably hungry. But not for C-rations.

In the center of the perimeter, Mort kept watch while Amos and Cooper slept. The mortar platoon was lucky to be positioned in the middle, but they still needed to be alert and prepared for anything. A few feet away was headquarters. One of the RTOs was always awake to get the sitrep hourly from each squad.

The bad part of being in the center was the dead were also there. Mort couldn't stop himself from occasionally glancing at the ponchos and thinking about Sanchez, Cal and CJ. He was tormented by the fact that if he hadn't been transferred to mortars, he might have been walking point. Mort recalled a quote from Shakespeare, *"If you prick us do we not bleed? If you tickle us do we not laugh? If you poison us do we not die? And if you wrong us shall we not revenge?"*

"I'm gonna get even, you yellow-bellied bastards!"

Amos took the second watch. The smell of rotten eggs made him gag. The poncho-wrapped bodies lay only a few feet away from him. He needed something to distract him. If only there was a full moon he could continue the letter to Judy. God, how he longed to see her! Their last night together kept replaying in his mind. She had laid her head on his shoulder. He could still feel the warmth of her breast against his arm and smell the floral scent of her perfume. She cried and softly sang to him: *"The moment I wake up, before I put on my makeup, I say a little prayer for you. While combing my hair now, and wondering what dress to wear now, I say a little prayer for you."*

Amos shut his eyes for only a second. He couldn't daydream. Out here you had to stay focused.

Brooklyn, JR, and Rico were in the next foxhole. Brooklyn was on watch. He was thinking about Cooper. He had been extremely quiet tonight. Brooklyn knew he was worried about Harris and Ferg. Tomorrow he would remind Cooper that they were the lucky ones because they were going home. He looked over at the ponchos laying only twenty feet away. CJ, Sanchez, and Cal would be going home too — in aluminum coffins. Maybe it was best to not say anything to Cooper. They would probably never find out more about Harris and Ferg. That was one of the difficult things — a friend was wounded, lifted out, and was never heard from again. You are expected to carry on as if nothing happened. It was a hell of a way to live.

At 0300 hours Fabe woke Brian. He was grateful to be able to get a little more sleep.

Since Brian's '60 had a bipod, it was already propped outside the foxhole ready to fire. Brian stepped up to his rifle and took over the watch. He was exhausted. Carrying Harris and humping the M60 was not easy. He was grateful for the sleep he had, but it wasn't nearly enough. His mind searched for a bible passage that would give him the strength he needed. *"He gives strength to the weary and increases the power of the weak."* That's what Isaiah said. Isaiah had plenty of problems and was no stranger to war. Yes, God would give him the strength he needed.

In the eerie stillness of the night his senses were heightened. The NVA were out there and they would probably attack. It was just a matter of time. At least tonight they were more prepared. He couldn't stop dwelling on the casualties they had taken. So many lives lost. So many wounded. He prayed they would make it out without further casualties. The Bible said not to hate, but how could you control that? After all, the Bible also says, *"An eye for an eye, a tooth for a tooth ... a wound for a wound."*

As he stared into the night, he scrutinized each branch and shadow. Each minute dragged on. The minutes turned into an hour.

The flash was so bright it nearly blinded him. Brian squinted and made out some figures low to the ground. Adrenaline flooded his system causing his heart to pound, almost exploding from his chest. He took a deep breath to steady himself and opened up with his M60. Within seconds, everyone on the north side of the perimeter was laying fire in the direction of the flare.

Fabe and Mex were instantly awake. Fabe could see the light from inside the foxhole. He closed one eye so his night vision wouldn't be totally gone. With one movement he grabbed his rifle and popped his head out of the foxhole, joining the others in showering the area of illumination with bullets.

Less than five minutes later everything was quiet except for men yelling for a medic. One man from the foxhole to Fabe's left had injuries to the shoulder and arm.

The whole company was awake and pumped with adrenaline. There would be no sleep the rest of the night.

The mortar platoon was in the center of the perimeter, so they couldn't see what was happening. Two images moved near them. They didn't need to see clearly to know it was Doc Bauer tending to the newly wounded man.

"Looks like we're down one more man." Chief spoke to Deadeye and Dan who were sharing his foxhole.

"I'd say we were damn lucky. If they'd attacked last night, we'd have been easy prey. We would've been lucky if one was left *alive.*" Dan emptied his fourth canteen.

"You better go easy on the water. Who knows when we'll get more." Deadeye wet his lips. He was rationing the water he had left.

"I have one canteen left. They gotta git them bodies out tomorrow. They'll bring food and water."

"Maybe. I'm sure glad we're in the center of the perimeter. I know they could break through our perimeter, but we're still a lot safer." Even though he was in the middle, Chief was ready if the NVA infiltrated the perimeter.

CHAPTER 8

The Wall

5 March 1969 – 0715 Hours

The platoon leaders met with Captain Hawk for their orders.

"TOC wants us to head south to an area where there have been several bomb strikes. They believe it will be clear enough to get in some choppers. Hopefully, we will get the wounded and dead out. They'll also be dropping off supplies. If that's successful, we will move east to provide reinforcement to Alpha Company. TOC believes Bravo will be able to join us by then."

"We'll proceed the same as yesterday: Second platoon leading, third platoon carrying the bodies and wounded, then mortars, and first platoon bringing up the rear."

At 0725 hours the men of Charlie Company started out. They were down to eighty-seven able men. The four wounded men were able to walk if assisted. Another twelve men would be carrying the bodies. Thirteen men would have double loads carrying the rucksacks and rifles of the wounded and dead men. That left only about fifty men able to move at the normal pace.

The sun was already hot when the third platoon resumed the duties of carrying the dead. Fabe picked up one end of a poncho, as Mex went to the other end. As they lifted it, their eyes met in horror as the body sagged to the middle. Mex turned his head as he emptied the contents of his stomach from the unanticipated smell of rotting flesh. Fabe gagged and swallowed the bile in his throat.

Neither man walked away from the job that had to be done. They picked up the body in silence as they took their place among the rest of the troop.

Deadeye stared at the third platoon carrying their load ahead of them. He turned to Brooklyn who was walking beside him. "I'm sure as hell glad to have the recoilless. At least I don't have to carry the bodies. It gives me the creeps to think about it. And I think the smell would make me puke."

Brooklyn nodded. "Those bodies smell like shit mixed wid rotten meat. I nuvah smelled anything like it. Didja eva? I mean, eva?"

"Never."

"Thank God I'm in mawhtas. Let the othuh platoons carry the poar fellas around."

After walking for an hour, the second platoon came to the base of a hill. Ten minutes later they came to a halt. The men in the back of the line hadn't even started up the incline.

"2-1 to Alpha 6."

"Go ahead, 2-1"

"Four-foot stone wall."

"Roger. Coming."

"Alpha 6 to all squads. Proceed to wall, stay low, and be ready." He didn't have to say more. They all knew he meant they should be ready for an ambush.

Everyone moved quickly and silently to the wall. Lil' Bro wiped sweat from his brow with his trembling hand. He couldn't believe his ears when Clark and Merdis volunteered to go over the wall first. As RTO he had to stay close to Merdis. That meant he would be the next one over.

The men of Charlie Company lined up along the wall, ready to provide cover. Fabe and Brian placed hand grenades on the wall in anticipation. Chief and Deadeye prepared the Recoilless.

"Brian, gimme your Pig." Merdis grabbed the M60 machine gun and an extra ammo belt.

Merdis and Clark stepped up to the wall and dropped their rucksacks. Clark slowly raised his M14. "I'll go over first."

"I'm right behind you!"

Clark cautiously raised his head to peak over the wall. He didn't see anything unusual, but he didn't expect to. If the NVA were laying in ambush, they would be well camouflaged.

Adrenaline flooded his system as he lifted himself to the top of the wall. In one movement he thrust himself over the wall, landed on the ground, and had his M14 ready to fire.

Silence.

Merdis followed.

As Merdis hit the ground a hailstorm of bullets landed all around him. Merdis and Clark reacted in a split second, as the thunderous sound of gunfire rang out from behind the wall. Clark's M14 rifle sent a burst of bullets into the wooded area ahead. Merdis held the trigger of the '60 down while shell casings flew to his right. The THA-Woooomp of the Recoilless resonated through the hillside.

Lil' Bro thought his heart might explode. When he had heard gunshots in movies, it only mildly increased his adrenaline. Out here it was like a shot of adrenaline directly into his veins. He froze.

The gunfire ended as quickly as it began.

"Holy Shit! You ok?"

"Ya! How the hell'd they miss us?" Merdis raised himself on his elbow.

Captain Hawk was the next person to jump the wall. He stopped and stared in disbelief. Merdis and Turner were alive and talking! "Second squad! Move out and search the area! Watch for booby traps!"

As the second platoon made their way up the hill, the rest of the company mounted the wall.

The mortar platoon needed to hoist High Angle Hell over the wall, and the third platoon had bodies to get over.

The men quickly organized themselves in bucket brigade fashion. Two men were posted on top of the wall, and four men on the other side. Rico and Dan transferred the baseplate and bipod for High Angle Hell by handing them to the men standing on the wall, who gave it to the men on the other side. They passed it on to JR and Mort, who carried it out of the way.

After High Angle Hell was over, Fabe and Mex stepped up to the wall. They lifted Cal's body to hand the poncho to the men on the wall. The body slumped in the middle, making it hard to lift it high enough. As they gave a heave to lift the body, an arm fell out of the poncho opening. The cold, green-black hand hit Fabe in the face. He gasped. A gold band on the blackened left finger gleamed in the sun. He felt paralyzed.

"Fabe!" Brian brought him back to action. Quickly, Fabe threw the cold arm back inside the poncho. When the man on top had a good hold on the poncho, he let out a sigh of relief. With clammy palms Fabe jumped over the wall. Biting his lip, he picked up one end of the poncho to take his place by the rest of his squad.

Fifteen minutes later, the second platoon returned. They had seen the area the recoilless had taken out. There was blood and lots of footprints. No sign of the NVA.

Hawk gave the signal for the men to move out.

The men had been walking for two hours when they stopped for a short break. There was no sign of the enemy since the ambush at the wall. The sun beat down relentlessly causing the smell from the ponchos to build.

Fabe and Mex were grateful to put down their load. Those carrying bodies placed them ten meters from where everyone was resting. The smell still carried to the group, but it was not as intense.

Mex took a swig from his canteen. "I'm sweating like a sinner in a church."

"We haveta get help carrying the poncho. It's too damn hard since the body's gone limp."

With more men, there would be two people on each end of the poncho making it considerably easier to carry.

"Brooklyn! We need help. Can you and Mort give us a hand when we go again?"

"I 'spose." Brooklyn emptied his fourth canteen. The last thing he wanted to do was help carry a body that smelled of decay. It was a horrible job, but it had to be done. "Damn that watta's good! I don't even care if it's hottah than piss. I sure as hell hope they bring mawh soon."

Cooper ran his fingers through his hair. "Me too. I'm already half through my last canteen, and it's hotter than seven hells out here." He was thinking he was grateful to be carrying the radio so he didn't have to carry a body. That would be about the worst job there was.

At 1100 hours they reached the clearing they had set out for. Captain Hawk called in for a dustoff to pick up bodies and wounded along with a request for ammo, food, water, and medical supplies. The bodies would be taken to Grave's Registration where they would be processed and sent home. The wounded would go to a field hospital.

While they were waiting for the dustoff, the men sat down at the edge of the clearing. If they stayed in the open area, they would be easy pickings. Hawk ordered half of the men to take guard duty while the others ate some rations and rested. "Platoon leaders, assign half of your squads to load men on the choppers. The other half will provide cover around the perimeter."

Brian, Mex, Fabe, and Lil' Bro took the first shift of guard duty. When they were relieved, they sat down.

After eating, Lil' Bro sat hugging his knees, his shoulders slumped, and head hung down. "Look at me. My new boots are covered with mud. My feet are still wet from the rice paddy. My clothes are covered with mud and blood. My shirt is wet with sweat. I'm exhausted. I'm scared... Jeez, I got a whole year ahead of me." "How am I gonna do it?"

"You learn to live with the fear. It doesn't go away. Every day is one less day until you go home." Home. Brian thought of his home in Illinois. He thought of his father, mother and younger brother. And Sara, the girl from church choir. The Sunday before he left, she had given him a small Bible to take with him. He touched his left pants pocket where he kept the Bible. Somehow, just touching the book gave him a feeling he was connected with her.

A few feet away, Deadeye finished his canned fruit. "Dan, how're your rations holding out?"

Dan was looking toward the bomb crater with the thousand-yard stare. He had seen so much. This was the worst he'd encountered in the nine months he'd been here. It was only day three in the field. Although they had been moving around, they weren't very far from where they started. They hadn't made any progress toward backing Alpha Company. They hadn't joined up with Bravo Company. There was nothing to show for the last three days except a tally of the dead and wounded. "What the hell for?"

"What?"

Dan broke his gaze and looked at Deadeye.

"Nothing. What'd you say?"

"How many cans of rations do you have left?"

"I don't know… not many. Three or four. I'm sure they'll be dropping water and rations when they get here." He hoped so. Right now, he wasn't sure of anything.

Amos finally had a few minutes to add a few more lines to his letter to Judy. He grabbed his paper and pencil out of the pocket of his pants. He was having trouble finding the right words.

Mort was sitting by Amos, staring at the ground. He was glad he helped carry the body of Cal. Somehow he felt like he was doing something for him. It wasn't much, but it felt good to bear some of the burden. Mort noticed Amos staring off into the distance. "You okay?

"I'm trying to find something to write to Judy. I can't keep telling her how bad it is."

"Write something nice — you don't have to always write about the war. Be romantic."

"I 'spose. I'm not very creative."

"Quote your favorite poem."

Amos chuckled. "I don't know any poems."

"That's ok, I can help. How 'bout a quote from Romeo and Juliet?

"My bounty is as boundless as the sea,
My love as deep; the more I give to thee
The more I have, for both are infinite.""

Amos started writing it down. "She'll know I got that from you, but it's ok. Good thing I have a buddy who loves Shakespeare."

Thirty minutes later they heard the dubdubdubdub of choppers approaching. Brian and Brooklyn grabbed a body-filled poncho and ran toward the approaching choppers. As the choppers descended, enemy fire broke out. The door gunners from the choppers returned fire, and the men of Charlie Company let loose. The choppers hoovered four feet from the ground. The men carrying the bodies picked up speed as they ran to the chopper.

Men from the first platoon helped the wounded men on the left side of the chopper.

Brian and Brooklyn were the last to upload their burden onto the right side of the chopper. They lifted the poncho to the door. Hitting the side of the chopper, the limp body fell out of the poncho.

Brian and Brooklyn turned ghastly white as the bloated green-black body of Sanchez fell to the ground.

Dropping the poncho, they frantically reached for Sanchez. Brooklyn grabbed his pant legs. As Brian grabbed his bare arms he felt something slimy in his hands. Without looking, he knew it was the skin peeling off. In a desperate measure to load the body, they took a firm grip and hoisted the body into the chopper as it began lifting up.

As soon as Sanchez was on the chopper it took off heading north. They would take the wounded men to the field hospital, then the bodies to Graves Registration.

Brian looked at the rotting flesh on his hands. His stomach contracted wanting to expel his guts. His stomach brought up bits of yellow bile, making him swallow hard. Grabbing for his canteen, he used some of his precious water to wash the remains of Sanchez off his hands.

When the helicopters were out of site, Brian sighed a breath of relief. *Praise the Lord! The choppers made it out of here with everyone loaded.* He turned to look for the supplies they dropped, desperate to refill his canteen.

He walked over to Fabe, who was crossing off another day on his calendar. "Where's the water?

"The pissers took off without dropping food. Only one jug of water — the first platoon grabbed it. And more ammunition."

"We gotta find a stream or rice paddy to fill the canteens. I'm practically out. My hands still smell of rotting flesh."

"My water's almost gone, too. At least we don't have to carry the bodies around anymore."

"Thank God for that. I think they sent back a guy who was short, too."

"He shouldn't have even come out with us. He has less than a week left before going home. "

"He didn't want to leave us. The Captain ordered him to go." Fabe respected Hawk for his decision. It was the right thing to do, even if it meant one less on their side.

Hawk met with the platoon and squad leaders. He informed them they would be heading east toward Alpha Company. Expect NVA ambushes. Third platoon walk point. Then first platoon, mortars, and second platoon.

The third platoon headed toward the jungle. It would

be foolish to take trails or clear areas. The NVA would have booby traps and ambushes set up along any path or clearing. The point man pushed his way through the thick brush and grasses occasionally using his machete to chop his way through the jungle. The machete was easier, but it was loud. They stayed near the edge of the jungle, so the foliage was not as heavy. Movement was still very slow.

After an hour of humping through the dense jungle, the Captain called for a break. They would be leaving the jungle and heading due east. The intense heat, leeches and mosquitoes were wearing on everyone.

Cautiously, they made their way to the jungle's edge. There they would take a break before they moved into the clearing. As the last man cleared the jungle, sniper fire broke out from two directions.

The men hit the ground. In a split second the sound of gunfire echoed through the hills. Again, the shooting stopped as quickly as it had begun. The snipers had left their mark, wounding two men. Doc did what he could but informed the captain that the wounds were life-threatening.

Since they were in a semi-clear area, Hawk called for an urgent dustoff accompanied by a gunship. Since it was critical to get these men out fast, there was no time to request supplies.

Fifteen minutes later two choppers approached. The gunship laid fire into the surrounding areas to provide some protection as the men loaded the wounded into the supply chopper.

Hawk was shocked when he saw a man jump off the chopper. He immediately recognized him as Major Close, who was part of the battalion headquarters.

In less than three minutes, the choppers had come and gone.

Hawk selected five men from the first platoon to scout the area ahead while he conversed with Major Close.

A new battalion commander had arrived that morning

to take over at TOC. He was determined to make more progress in getting Charlie Company connected with Alpha Company. He wanted faster results, including updated reports on the NVA presence in the area. It did not help the situation that Charlie Company was not close to making contact with Bravo Company, either. He had sent Major Close into the field to be a presence on the ground.

When the first platoon had returned from scouting, they reported heavy signs of NVA to the east.

Captain Hawk redirected the men to head south-east. He needed to get his troops to a relatively safe area before dusk fell. The sky was clouded over, providing much needed relief from the scorching sun. Rain was likely. It would feel so good to have even a sprinkle of water. The men needed a break from the intense heat. Often a blessing is a curse. They needed time to dig in for the night. The blackness of the night would give the NVA a big advantage. He did not want a repeat of their first night in the field – especially on a night the moon was not out.

By 1700 hours they were digging foxholes and setting up tripwires in the surrounding area. A fine mist fell, giving them a cool relief from the heat.

An hour later the men were settled in their foxholes. The mist had turned into a light rain.

"It's darker than Hades out here." Brian had the first watch tonight.

"At least we got the dead and wounded out. I'm getting some shut eye." Fabe pulled his poncho over his head as he leaned against the dirt wall of his foxhole.

Brian strained to see into the darkness. The night was as dark as a bushel of blackbirds at midnight. No moon. You couldn't see your hand if you waved it in front of your face. He could hear the sound of metal hitting ground or rock. The NVA was digging in. They were out there somewhere. But where? He didn't know how they could work in the pitch black. The sound ground on his nerves. The rain had provided a welcome reprieve from the heat, but it made the smell of the dried blood and stinky rice paddy water worse. It reminded him of rotting garbage. At least he didn't have to listen to the moans of wounded men. Thank God.

Major Close was next to Captain Hawk in the center of the perimeter. He hung up his radio handset. "The call was from Brigade. They want us to move north tonight to the blocking position."

"That's at least two kilometers – maybe more!" This meant going back to the area they had been in earlier.

"They're not happy with your progress. They want you to get to Alpha Company NOW."

"We'd have to cut back through the jungle. The NVA thrive in the night." Thoughts raced through Hawk's head. *Couldn't he hear them digging in around us? We weren't able to move in that direction during the daylight. Moving now would be a suicide mission.* "We'd take heavy casualties. There's no way we could get a Medivac in. Hell! We couldn't get the guys out in the daylight for two days."

"The Brigade Commander has given the order himself!"

Hawk was silent. He was caught between a rock and a hard place. Going against a direct order was unthinkable. He had always carried out his orders, no matter how difficult the situation was. If he refused to move on tonight, the consequences would be severe. If he obeyed orders it would be a suicide mission. He was responsible for his men. How could he do this to them?

Captain Hawk shook his head. Whatever the repercussions were, he'd have to face it. "No. I'm not moving. I know it's unheard of to refuse to follow an order, but I can't do it. We're already down twenty men. That's nearly one-fourth of our company. I know we'd take heavy casualties with no way to get them out. It would be a suicide mission. I just can't do it."

Major Close was silent for two full minutes. He knew Hawk had a lot of experience in Vietnam and was aware of the ramifications of such a decision. He was sent to the field to see that orders were carried out and progress made. Yet, he realized Hawk was right. If they moved tonight, it was possible none of them would see daylight again. "Ok. I'm with you. I'm the senior officer on the ground. I'll say it's my decision."

After talking to TOC, Major Close turned to Captain Hawk. "The Brigade Commander is furious. He says he's coming out right now to relieve me and take charge."

CHAPTER 9

Walking Point

6 March 1969 – 0700 Hours

Captain Hawk was relieved the drizzling rain had stopped. "Well, Major, no show for the Brigade Commander."

"I talked to TOC. Apparently the chopper pilot started out, but he turned back. He refused to fly into this area last night. Too dark and rainy. I bet it's hell to pay for him."

"You'll be in deep shit when you get back, too. But we made the right decision. We're already down twenty men."

Major Close nodded in agreement. "Let's hope we can avoid any casualties today."

"We'll start out deeper in the jungle. It'll give us more protection."

The men were eating rations and preparing to move out. Brooklyn took a bite of cold, slimy, grey-colored eggs. "Well, you'se guys made it anudda day."

"Ya. I 'spose I'll get used to it." Cooper took a drink from his canteen.

"You nevah get used to it. Let's see the picture of your girlfriend."

"I told you. She's NOT my girlfriend. Just a friend."

"Ok. Let's see the picture of your girl. FRIEND."

Cooper took a photo out of his wallet and handed it to Brooklyn. "Her name is Peggy."

"Holy shit! That's not what I was expectin!" Brooklyn had an evil smile on his face.

Cooper chuckled and for the first time since he'd been in the field, he felt relaxed and even a little happy. "She's a looker."

"A looka? She makes Raquel Welch look ugly." "Hey, JR! Looky here!"

Rico followed JR as he walked over to Brooklyn. "Whatcha got?"

Brooklyn handed JR the picture. JR's mouth curved into a broad smile. "Who's the bombshell?"

"It's Peggy. Cooper's FRIEND."

Rico grabbed the picture as he stared at Peggy. She had long, flowing, voluminous blonde hair. Her sparkling blue eyes were accentuated with black cats-eye liner. Her full, red lips were slightly parted. She was a goddess in her low-cut dress. Rico let out a cat call.

Cooper's laugh was interrupted by a signal from Hawk to get ready to move out. "Gimme my picture!"

"I suppose my wife wouldn't approve of me keeping it, anyway."

Cooper carefully put the picture of Peggy back in his wallet. It was true she was not his girlfriend, but he still treasured the picture she gave him. Besides his mom and dad, she was the only other person who had sent him a letter. Her beauty went way beyond her looks. She had a heart of gold. After running his fingers through his dirty hair, he put on his helmet and bent to pick up his rucksack.

At 0745 hours the company was ready to move on. Again, the third platoon was to take the lead. Brian saw Merdis and Clark having a serious discussion. Merdis was rubbing the nape of his neck as he and Clark approached Brian. He dreaded what was coming next.

"Brian, we're going first. Your turn to walk point."

"Ok." Brian took a deep breath as he looked at the map Merdis was carrying.

Merdis pointed to a position north-east of their night lager. "It's the same general direction y'all retreated from yesterday. By now the NVA have figured out we're tryin' to help Alpha Co. They'll be watchin' the area close, so we'll have to take a new path deeper into the jungle. Y'all will have to chop your way through." Merdis handed a compass to Brian.

"I don't have a machete."

"Take mine." Merdis unclipped the swivel hook from his belt and handed Brian his machete in its sheath. "Fabe and Mex will be right behind you. I'll follow them."

Brian walked over to Fabe. "I'm walking point. You want the '60?"

"Sure." Fabe handed Brian his M16 in exchange. The '60 was too heavy and bulky for Brian to carry while using the machete. Brian was good at walking point, but that didn't stop Fabe from worrying about his friend. "Good luck."

The heat of the sun on the damp ground made it feel like a sauna. Brian wanted to gulp some water before starting out, but he knew he had to ration it. He had only half of a canteen left. He said a prayer before starting out, as he did every day. *God, thank you for keeping me safe so far. Help me through this day. Help me to see signs of danger. Amen.*

As Brian entered the jungle he was on high alert. His eyes darted from side to side scanning for anything that might be an indication of NVA presence. The jungle was so thick he had to cut his way through most of the time. He held his machete with his right hand, and carried the borrowed M16 under his left arm. Its barrel was constantly getting tangled in the jungle's dense undergrowth. He had to take high steps to keep from tripping on the roots laying on the jungle floor. Beads of sweat were dripping down his back. The work was exhausting. He was so thirsty! He saw a smooth stone and picked it up to suck on.

The jungle had a way of increasing your anxiety. Brian couldn't see two feet ahead. He had to constantly reference the compass to know he was going in the right direction. Plants, leaves, and animal decay on the jungle floor made it difficult to detect any booby traps or spider holes. This wasn't a likely place for a booby trap, but you couldn't be too careful. The mosquitoes and leeches were constantly assaulting him. The sound of the machete might be heard by the enemy. Fear coursed through his veins. He felt as though he was being pulled by an invisible thread. *I have to keep calm.* Again, he prayed for guidance as he searched his mind for something comforting. *"Surely it is God who saves me. I will trust in him and not be afraid."* His breathing slowed. He moved forward, knowing God was with him.

The progress was slow. Brian let out a sigh of relief as they reached the destination at the edge of the jungle after two hours of exhausting work.

"I'll talk to the captain and get the coordinates from here." Merdis took the handset from Lil' Bro's radio and updated Hawk on their progress.

After getting his orders, Merdis pointed north. "We'll head through the open area toward the rice paddy in the distance. Y'all go in the grassy area to wait for the rest of the guys to clear the jungle. We'll take twenty before we head out."

Lil' Bro was sitting next to Brian and Fabe. "At least it should be easy going now that we're out of the jungle."

Brian looked at Lil' Bro. He was so young and naive. "Actually, it's worse walking point in the open. It's hard work, cutting a path through the jungle, but it's also not likely you'll run into a booby trap there. It's much more dangerous if you're on a path or out in the open. The NVA might be waiting anywhere in ambush. There's so much to look out for — booby traps of all kinds. Wires, punji sticks, mines, Bouncing Bettys. The tripwires and mines are put in places they think we're likely to walk. It's not bad enough they're made to hurt or kill us, but then the NVA knows exactly where we are."

"Aren't Bouncing Bettys landmines?"

Fabe shook his head as he joined in the conversation. "No. Yes. Well, there are a lot of different land mines.

Bouncing Bettys are the worst. So, we kinda put them into a separate category."

"I don't get it."

"Bouncing Betty is the mine we fear most. It's hard to spot and it's deadly."

"Aren't they all deadly?"

"They can be. But Bouncing Betty is worse."

"Why?"

Brian loved teaching cherries like Lil' Bro. "Well, like any mine, it's hard to spot. There're three prongs that stick up above the ground. If there's a little grass, it's impossible to see. You don't know when you step on it, but when you take the next step it explodes. It won't go off until the pressure is off it. It'll fly up for three feet or more. Hundreds of pieces of shrapnel, scrap metal, and ball bearings fly in all directions. It can kill someone up to 100 meters away."

"I thought it would be easier now. Somehow, things only keep getting worse."

Cooper sat down next to Brooklyn. There was tall grass all around them, and very little scrub brush. The grass was cool and damp. They could see at least 1000 meters to the north. Cooper dropped his rucksack with the radio and took a small swig of his water. He had only a couple swallows remaining in the canteen. He pointed to a dip in the horizon. "Looks like there's a rice paddy over there. I hope there's a stream nearby where we can get some water."

"Me, too."

Cooper took off his helmet and ran his fingers through his dirty hair. "I'm almost out."

"Holy shitballs!" Brooklyn's eyes were as big as saucers. He pointed to the edge of the jungle where they had been ten minutes earlier. "There goes a fuckin' gook!"

"Where? I don't see him." Cooper dropped his canteen and grabbed for his rifle.

"He ducked back into the jungle."

Cooper squinted. It was easy to disappear in the jungle foliage. His heart was pounding as he cradled his rifle in his arms. "Do ya think he was behind us all the while?"

"Creepy, ain't it? They's sneaky sons 'o bitches." Brooklyn kept staring at the jungle. Maybe he imagined it. Maybe he was getting delirious.

Cooper was thinking the same thing. Maybe Brooklyn was seeing things. Cooper changed the subject. "I sure as hell wish they would drop us some food and water. I'm about out of both."

"Look!" Brooklyn pointed toward the jungle.

This time Cooper saw an NVA soldier ducking back into the jungle. This was no delusion. The reality was that the NVA were watching their movement. He looked around at his comrades. Others were pointing to the jungle. He felt sick. He quickly forgot he was hungry.

Dan and Deadeye both saw Brooklyn and Cooper pointing. Deadeye stared in disbelief. "Those motherfuckers have been following us all morning."

"This whole mountain is crawling with NVA. What the hell are they up to?"

"I doan know, but we bettah watch our backs."

Merdis walked over to Brian. "Hawk informed me that there have been several gooks spotted in the jungle behind us." Merdis took out his map. "He decided to change our direction a little. Instead of going in the open, we'll be heading into the jungle 120 meters to the northwest. Let's move out."

Brian's nerves were on edge going through the open field that led to the area where they would enter the jungle. The chances of an attack or finding a booby trap were high. The fact that the NVA were at the edge of the jungle they had just came through made him fear they had a plan in mind. His hands trembled as he felt the responsibility of leading the men to safety. He was almost to the jungle's edge when he heard the dreaded hiss of incoming mortars, mingled with the crack of the AK47. He broke into a run to reach the cover of the jungle. "INCOMING!"

His words were echoed throughout the line of men as they frantically searched for even the smallest bit of cover. Fabe, Mex, Merdis, and the rest of the third platoon followed Brian's lead and scrambled toward the cover of the jungle.

Mortars and the second platoon were farther behind. The first round struck to their right. Amos and Brooklyn instinctively dove for a small dip in the ground to their left. The men carrying the large pieces of High Angle Hell dropped their loads and followed Amos and Brooklyn. The second platoon scrambled in the same direction. They all hunkered close to the ground with their hands over their heads as mortar rounds continued to land off to their right.

The first platoon was bringing up the rear. The mortars were landing toward their right, and sniper fire had broken out from behind them. They had nowhere to go, so they hit the ground and began firing in the direction of the NVA. Someone launched a M79 grenade in hopes of disabling the men firing the AK47s.

Hawk had taken cover in the jungle. He grabbed the radio and requested artillery fire to knock out the NVA mortar tube. After five mortar rounds landed, there was a lull, then two more mortar rounds landed closer to them before the requested artillery met its mark and stopped the incoming.

Mort heard men crying out in panic. As Mort lifted his head to look around, he could see none of his buddies were hit. Again, the mortar platoon was spared. As he looked farther down beyond the shallow ravine, he could see where the screaming and swearing was coming from. The men in the second platoon were not so lucky. While the first five rounds were off target, the last two landed close enough to injure four men. He saw Hawk, Doc Bauer, and the other medics running to the wounded.

Doc didn't have to tell Captain Hawk how bad some of the men were wounded. He could see for himself he would need to call for an urgent dustoff. Too many men had already been lost on this mission. He would not request supplies as some of the men's lives depended on getting to the field hospital quickly.

After contacting TOC, Captain Hawk met with the platoon leaders. "First and third platoon spread out to provide cover from all directions when the choppers come in. Mortars and second platoon load the wounded."

Ten minutes later a chopper accompanied by a gunship were on their way. They managed to get the wounded out without receiving any enemy fire.

At 1130 hours Brian entered the jungle. *God, please help me safely lead these men today. Haven't we suffered enough casualties? Please guide me and keep us safe.*

Brian began his difficult task of chopping his way through the jungle and diligently watching for any signs of trouble. He let out a sigh of relief when he reached the jungle's edge at 1300 hours. Merdis quickly stepped up beside him. He grabbed the handset of the radio carried by Lil' Bro.

"3-2 to Alpha 6."

"Go ahead 3-2."

"We've reached our destination."

"Find a place to wait for the rest of the guys to catch up."

"10-4 and out."

It took twenty minutes before the last man was out of the jungle. The men were grateful to take a break in the heat of the day.

Lil' Bro sat down next to Doc Bauer. He looked as if he was ready to drop over. His clothes were covered with dried blood. His eyes were dark and sunken in. "I hope you get a little rest tonight. You look like hell."

"I'm ok."

"Why don't you have a drink of water?"

"My water's gone."

Lil' Bro had seen Doc use his own water supply to give to the wounded and to clean their wounds. "Then have a little of mine."

Doc gratefully took a small swig from Lil' Bro's canteen. Lil' Bro studied Doc. "How come you don't carry a gun?"

"I'm a conscientious objector. My religious beliefs don't allow me to kill. But I felt the need to serve when most of my friends were drafted. So, I enlisted as a conscientious objector. A lot of the medics are conscientious objectors."

"Oh. I don't know if I can kill anyone, either."

Hawk hung up the handset of his radio. He turned to Major Close. "I got orders to advance the men to the area on the other side of the rice paddy. TOC said Bravo Company will join us today."

"Do you really think we'll join up with Bravo?"

"Well, Sir, they'll try to get to us. This place is crawling with NVA. I suspect they'll do all they can to keep us from joining forces."

CHAPTER 10

NVA Everywhere

1330 Hours

The third platoon again took the lead because of the heavy casualties taken by the first and second platoons. Brian was relieved when Merdis told him he would not have to walk point again.

That was not good news for Mex. It was his turn. As Mex stood up to go to the front of the line a chill went down his spine. This was the moment he was dreading. As he stepped in front of Brian, one of the men from another squad walked past him. "I'm walking point."

Mex knew some guys liked to walk point, but he couldn't believe anyone would volunteer on this mission. "What?"

"Are you deaf? I said I was walking point."

Mex let out a sigh of relief. He couldn't believe his good luck. Quickly, he stepped in line behind the point man.

Staying as close to the jungle as they could, the men proceeded cautiously. It wasn't long before they had to veer into the open to get to their destination. Staying strung out in a line, they kept three meters between each person. There was no protection from the sun as they made their way into the open field.

It was 1400 hours when Clark screamed, "INCOMING!" Because they were in the open there was no cover for anyone in Charlie Company. No sooner than they had heard the hiss of the mortar, rifle fire broke out from the tree line of the jungle. The NVA had been waiting for them to enter this area, as Captain Hawk had feared. Since the forward observer had been diligent in tracking their coordinates, Captain Hawk immediately called for artillery.

Artillery responded quickly. But not soon enough. This time the NVA had done a better job of sighting in their mortars. Before the mortar fire stopped, Doc Bauer was running to the wounded men. The other medics followed his lead. Doc Bauer quickly assessed the situation. Six men were wounded. The seventh victim did not need a medic.

Since it was quiet at the moment, Hawk requested an urgent dustoff. It was a good place to land a chopper. He prayed they would be able to get the wounded out. Some of the injuries were very serious. It would also be extremely dangerous to proceed with the seventy-four remaining men if they had to transport the dead and wounded.

TOC responded. They would send gunships to accompany the chopper to evacuate the dead and wounded soldiers. If they received too much enemy fire, they would turn back. They could not afford to lose any more helicopters or men.

Captain Hawk moved the men one hundred meters back in the direction they came from so they would have some protection in a shallow ravine. While they waited, he ordered half the company to stand watch.

Brian spotted Mex sitting off to the side holding his head in his hands. He walked over to him and sat down. Mex didn't even notice he was there. Brian sat by him and remained silent. After a couple of minutes Brian couldn't stand it any longer. He put his hand on his shoulder. "What happened? You ok?"

Mex slowly raised his head and stared into the distance. "I'm alive. I guess that makes me ok, doesn't it?"

"Talk to me, bro."

"The guy who was walking point took bullets from the AK47. He's dead."

"Thank God it wasn't you."

"Damn it, Brian! Don't you see? I WANTED him to walk point. I didn't wanna die. Now he's dead, and it's my fault."

"It's not your fault."

"But I have to live with it — knowing he died because of me."

"It's all part of God's plan. You gotta let it go."

"I don't know if I can."

Mort was sitting next to Amos, while Brooklyn and Cooper kept watch. Amos gobbled a can of C-rations and took out his picture of Judy. "You got any more poems? I still don't know what to write to Judy."

Mort smiled. "Sure, I have enough to fill pages and pages."

"Man, you must really love poetry."

"I love the theater. I plan to go into acting when I get back to the world."

"Ta heck! I thought you wanted to be a doctor like your old man."'

"No. My old man wanted me to be a doctor. If I wanted to be a doctor, I'd be in college now with a student deferment."

"You're my best buddy, and I didn't even know that."

"Well, don't broadcast it. Some of these guys think actors are sissies."

"As long as you keep feeding me lines to write to Judy, I'll keep your secret." "What's your favorite?"

"Shakespeare:

"Life's but a walking shadow, a poor player
That struts and frets his hour upon the stage
And then is heard no more: it is a tale
Told by an idiot, full of sound and fury
Signifying nothing.""

"Macbeth?"

"Yes. I didn't know you liked Shakespeare."

"I don't. They made us read Macbeth in high school."

Deadeye and Dan were enjoying a cigarette as Chief kept watch. Deadeye snuffed out his cigarette butt. "I got one cigarette left."

Dan handed Deadeye a four-pack of Marlboro. "I got more. I traded my coffee with Chief and Rico for cigarettes."

"You're the best damned buddy a guy could have."

"Sure, you say that now. We'll see what you say when those cigarettes are gone." Dan laughed. He and Deadeye were tight. Nothing could break up their friendship.

Lil' Bro was sitting next to Fabe watching the sky for the approach of the choppers. As Fabe marked another day off his calendar, Lil' Bro took off his C scarf and wiped his brow.

"Will they bring in water and food when they come?"

"I sure as hell hope so."

"What if they don't?"

"Maybe we can get some water from the rice paddy up ahead."

"I don't know if I can drink that smelly water. It's full of bugs and God only knows what else."

"Put a couple of iodine tablets in it and add Kool-Aid to help cover up the taste. It still tastes bad, but it helps. Anyway, it's wet and it keeps you alive."

"Great. One more thing to add to the list of ways to kill us – drinking stinky, dirty water full of bugs."

At 1440 hours Lil' Bro saw two choppers appear on the horizon. All the men, except those who were waiting to load the wounded, raised their weapons ready to defend their perimeter. By 1447 hours the dustoff was completed without incident. No food or water was brought in.

The remaining men of Charlie Company proceeded to make their way toward the distant rice paddy. By 1540 hours they could see the rice paddy within reach, causing them to unconsciously pick up their pace. The scorching afternoon sun beat down. Ahead were a few small trees and some tall grass. This was the most cover they had seen in the last hour, so they stopped. Captain Hawk looked at his watch. He would request a gunship to come in and discourage the NVA before they proceeded to the rice paddy. "We'll take forty-five. Split into groups of three. Each man keeps watch for fifteen minutes. Chow down. Have a cigarette. We should still make it to our destination early enough to dig in."

Clark kept watch while Lil' Bro and Merdis ate their rations. Merdis, like Fabe, felt he needed to keep watch over Lil' Bro. He had assigned him to the radio so he would be close. "Ration your water."

"Ya, I know. Why didn't they bring in food and water when they picked up the wounded?"

"God only knows. I'm sure it created chaos when Colonel Stinson was killed. Maybe that's why they can't get their shit together. We're the poor bastards who're suffering."

As Lil' Bro took a swig from his canteen he looked at Merdis, then Clark. They were one hell of a duo. They were fierce combat soldiers. But they were also great guys. No wonder everyone in their platoon respected them.

Clark and Brian sat down next to Lil' Bro when Merdis and Fabe took over guard duty. Clark grabbed a can of C rations. "Merdis thinks he's smart. He told me an onion is the only food that makes you cry. So I threw a can of C Rations in his face." Clark laughed at his own joke.

"Good one." Brian loved Clark's jokes.

Lil' Bro smiled. He knew he was lucky to be in a unit where the men got along so well.

Brian took out his Kodak camera and took a picture of the rice paddy that was their destination. He always tried to capture moments that had meaning to him. He sent the film home and his mother had it developed. Until now, he'd been too busy to even think about pictures. He'd try to get more on this mission – it definitely was one he wasn't going to forget.

After twenty minutes a gunship appeared, as requested by Captain Hawk. The gunship had fired only a few rounds when it began smoking. NVA automatic weapon fire had hit their target again.

"Geez Louise!" Fabe watched the aircraft slowly descend as it went off into the horizon. "There goes our air support."

The whole company became deadly silent. It looked like they were jumping out of the frying pan into the fire.

An hour later they reached their destination without any casualties. Hawk signaled for the men to spread out, stay low, and stop fifty meters south of the paddy. The NVA could be anywhere. He walked to the top of a nearby knoll. His trained eyes scanned his surroundings.

A stream ran into the far end of a narrow rice paddy. There was a dike down the center of the paddy, running north and south. TOC had ordered them to go past the paddy and stay there. It would put them in a blocking position to protect Alpha Company from an attack from the south. At any rate, there was no turning back as they had seen numerous NVA at the edge of the jungle behind them.

Captain Hawk scanned the area north of the paddy. That was where they were supposed to set up their night lager. They would have to run along the dike to get there.

On the east side of the rice paddy, there was a ridge resembling a sugarloaf. He could see three men in uniforms walking around on the ridge. It would be a hot attack as they crossed the dike. They had no choice but to continue on as TOC ordered. He had disobeyed orders once. He would not do it again.

The platoon and squad leaders had joined him. Merdis took a position next to Captain Hawk. "Sir, we spotted several NVA behind us. I'm sure there's more. We have to keep going forward."

"You're right. We have no choice. You lead the way."

Merdis shook his head. "I don't mean to be disrespectful, Sir, but I don't want to be responsible."

Captain Hawk took a deep breath. *I don't need this right now. I have to come up with a plan.*

After only a minute's silence, Captain Hawk turned to Merdis. "If we don't get moving, we're going DEROS right now. Will you go if I send Turner with you?"

"Yes, Sir. I'll go with Clark."

"Okay. Third Platoon will follow you. We'll go across the dike single file. As soon as you start out, I'll get some smoke going to cover you."

Hawk turned to his first sergeant. "Give the orders to proceed. Have the men put their bayonets on their rifles. Who knows where the NVA will pop up? There may be hand-to-hand combat."

"Sir, I don't believe the men have their bayonets with them."

"Damn it! What else can go wrong?"

Merdis and Clark led the third platoon to the edge of the rice paddy by the dike. Merdis took charge. "Clark will go first. Then me. The rest of you follow, single file. Keep crouched down and dart across as fast as you can. Spread out so you don't make yourselves easy targets. Those NVA will be trying to pick us off, so fire across the paddy as you go. No pausing anywhere. I know you're outta water, but this is not the time to try to fill your canteen. As soon as we take off Hawk will get some smoke going."

Clark flashed his teeth, threw his head back, and let out a battle cry as he lunged forward. "EEEEEiiiiiiaaaaaaa!

Pausing only a second, Merdis followed as Hawk's first sergeant detonated a smoke bomb.

Lil' Bro jumped up on the dike and followed after Merdis, adrenaline flooding his system. He kept his eyes on the path, never looking up to see the NVA that were sending lead in his direction.

A feeling of dread crept up from the pit of his stomach as Fabe scrambled onto the dike after Lil' Bro. His eyes watered from the smoke in the air. His rifle fired in the general direction of the NVA, with no specific target in mind. Brian followed, continually repeating, "Please, God. Please."

Hawk and the second platoon went next, followed by the Mortars and what was left of the first platoon.

Before the last man had stepped onto the dike, Clark had reached the other side unscathed. As he took his last step off the dike, he spotted an NVA officer to his right. It seemed as though he came out of nowhere. Raising his pistol, he shouted, "BAN DA CHET!"

With lightning speed, Clark's rifle exploded putting a hole in the officer's skull. Merdis rushed past him, leading the men to safety. Clark grabbed the Tokarev pistol with a star on its handle grip as his war trophy. Since his clothing indicated he was an officer, Clark checked his pockets. Officers often had some kind of papers regarding their mission. In his left inside pocket, he felt something bulky. Reaching inside the pocket, he grabbed the paper documents. Then, pausing for only a second, he took his C scarf and placed it over the officer's face like a shroud. "Charlie Company is here. We'll send you all straight to hell."

The mortar platoon stepped onto the dike. Cooper had been intently watching the men in the third and second platoons cross. It appeared as if every third person was getting targeted by the NVA. While waiting for his turn to cross the dike, Cooper counted the people in front of him. He made sure he wasn't going to be number three. Right ahead of him was Dan and Rico. Since they were carrying pieces of High Angle Hell, they put their heads down and ran. *Here goes nothing!* He raised his rifle as he stepped onto the dike. Running as fast as he could, he began blindly firing at the NVA. He was feeling pretty confident he'd make it across. If his calculations were right, he wasn't in jeopardy. When he was only one-third of the way across the dike, he was doubting his calculations. Bullets were flying everywhere. He picked up his speed as bullets hit the ground millimeters from his feet.

When the men of the mortar platoon were safely on the other side, Cooper stopped near Clark to catch his breath. He looked at Clark in astonishment. Clark was watching him and laughing.

Cooper was pissed off. "What the hell are you laughing at?"

"You looked like the fuckin' roadrunner in cartoons. Your legs from the knees down looked like wheels."

When all the men were across the dike, they gathered near some scrub brush, out of range of the NVA. They would wait there to get orders from Hawk.

Hawk never understood how the entire company made it across the dike without any casualties. The men were pumped with adrenaline, and he paused to listen to some of the conversations taking place.

"Madre de Dios! I made it!"

"Did you see how many were out there?"

"How the hell'd they miss us?"

"I hit at least one of the bastards!"

Hawk turned his attention to his surroundings. To his left was a crumbling three-foot stone wall. It looked as if it had been part of a dike from the past. The wall was located at the base of a small hill. On this side of the wall was grass and some scrub brush. The hill itself was barren — he could see it had been bombed. To the left, beyond the wall, was the edge of a jungle. To the right was scrub brush, then the small, narrow stream flowing into the rice paddy. This was the area Brigade ordered them to set up a blocking position.

Merdis and Clark walked over to Hawk to get the next orders. The other platoon and squad leaders did the same. Clark handed the documents to Hawk. "I found these on the NVA officer I shot."

"Nice work. I'm glad you thought to check his pockets. Was there anything else on him?"

"Just his pistol. But I ain't givin' that up."

Hawk turned to the men who were waiting for orders. "Start digging fox holes and secure the area we're in. Dig in deep. We might be here for a while. First platoon and mortars in the middle, behind the wall. Headquarters will also be there. Third platoon to the right, second platoon to the left. Stay close together. I know you're low on water, but stay away from the stream. The NVA has a clear view of that area, and I don't want any more casualties. START DIGGING!"

The men went to their designated areas. Most foxholes were dug to accommodate three men. One man kept watch while the others worked on digging the hole. There were still a couple of hours of daylight, so there was plenty of time to dig deep and set up a perimeter.

The mortar platoon was setting up next to the third platoon, but had a little extra shelter from the dike wall. Amos, Mort, Dan, and Rico set up High Angle Hell before they started digging. Next to them Deadeye and Chief were checking the recoilless.

Mort smiled. "I guess another advantage of being with mortars is that we set up in the middle."

JR was keeping watch for their group. "That's right. You're lucky you got transferred to the mortar platoon, because in the mortar platoon nobody's been killed since I've been here."

Mort gave no reply. Once again, his thoughts went to Sanchez, Cal, and CJ. He replayed the same scenario over and over in his mind. He could still hear Sanchez laugh as he was beating him in poker the last night they were on LZ Professional. Then, the look he had at the helipad. Then, the eyes staring into nothingness. The stare of death. *Why? Why was I transferred to mortars? Why wasn't it me? If I had stayed in the first platoon I might have been walking point. CJ would be alive, and I'd be in paradise with Sanchez.*

"Mort! You ok?"

Mort blinked and shook his head. His thoughts returned to the present. "Ya. I'm ok." His best friend was Amos. JR said no one had been killed in the mortar platoon. Thank God. He didn't know what he would do if something happened to Amos, too.

Merdis, Lil' Bro and Doc Bauer were sharing a foxhole. Brian, Fabe and Mex were in the hole next to them.

Lil' Bro stopped to wipe sweat with his C scarf. "I don't know where Merdis went. He told me to start diggin'."

"Oh, for cryin' out loud. He'll be back to help. And if he's not, we'll help you." Brian was on watch.

Fabe smiled. "Somebody has to help you. You're too short to dig deep."

"Ha. Ha. You're real funny, Fabe."

Hawk called in to TOC to request a drop of water and food. The request was denied due to the heavy NVA presence in the area. He turned to Major Close. "I really thought they'd bring in supplies. Especially after I told them we had documents. At least they agreed to send a Spooky in tonight. Hopefully, that will make it possible to get re-supplied in the morning."

"I can't believe they didn't come get the documents right away. It must be bad everywhere."

Major Close was right. Back at TOC everything was in chaos. Colonel Stinson's replacement was new to the command. One of the other senior officers left because it was the end of his tour of duty. All the brigades in the Americal division were receiving heavy casualties. There were no reinforcements left. Two-thirds of the division's helicopters had been shot down. Tin Phouc was constantly being assaulted, drawing heavy casualties. Every day new NVA bunkers and tunnels were discovered. Some days as many as thirty bunkers were spotted by air control in one fly-around. Alpha, Bravo, and Charlie Company were all receiving heavy fire. Casualties were increasing at an alarming rate. Delta Company was struggling to keep control of LZ Professional. The 1/52 was in danger of being overrun. Every time a chopper attempted to land at Professional to pick up supplies they received enemy fire. The firebase was under almost constant attack the last two days, and the casualties there were starting to mount up. In addition, because of the positions of Alpha, Bravo, and Charlie Companies, it was becoming difficult to impact the NVA with the Spooky without taking out their own men.

When TOC denied Captain Hawk's request, they did not give him the details. It was true, the NVA surrounding Charlie Company was making it difficult to deliver supplies. But that was just the tip of the iceberg.

CHAPTER 11

Digging In

1900 Hours

The seventy-four men of Charlie Company dug foxholes deeper than ever before. They were spaced six to eight feet apart in a checkerboard pattern. Claymores and trip wires were set up around the perimeter. High Angle Hell was set up, and Headquarters was located close by.

As Captain Hawk stood in his foxhole, he studied his surroundings. Behind him was the old dike wall. It had seen better days, but it still gave them some cover. Beyond the wall was an open hill free of vegetation. There had obviously been a significant battle there before. Looking at the bomb crater and the fox holes in that area, he presumed the NVA had been dug in and were bombed by the US. Or American troops had been dug in and were bombed by the NVA. To his right, beyond the second platoon, lay the jungle. They would need to keep a close watch in that area, as it would be easy for the NVA to sneak up on them. He turned to look in the direction of the dike they had crossed. NVA were scattered everywhere, as if they intentionally made their presence known. Why? To instill fear in his men? Farther to the left, beyond the rice paddy, was a sugarloaf. There he could also see NVA. They were in groups – a group of twenty, a group of thirty, a group of fifteen. They were marching – communist kind of strutting marching. *Give me a break! It's like they're in a garrison area. They're everywhere. My God! How many are out there?* They had certainly seen Charlie Company come across the dike. If he could see the NVA, the NVA could see him. It was a big concern that they were so willing to show themselves. At this end of the rice paddy, 200 meters from the third platoon, ran a small stream. He would pass the word to the platoon leaders to warn the men not to go near the stream. It was way too dangerous. In the morning he would request supplies again. They needed to get water in before some desperate man tried to get water from the stream.

According to the coordinates he received from headquarters, Hawk realized they were only about two kilometers from Alpha Company. They had been pinned down in the same area for several days.

Major Close stood beside Captain Hawk. "Well, TOC should be happy. We managed to get to the position they want us in."

"Yes, Sir. I'm sure it looks great on the map they have at brigade headquarters. If they were out here, it would look different. There are plenty of other ways for the NVA to continue their attack on Alpha Company. The problem is, we have nowhere to go. We're surrounded on three sides. Our only choice is to go up the hill where there is no cover. They'll be ready for us to make our move in that direction."

"It's a possibility, Hawk. On the bright side, it is fairly secure as long as we stay by this wall. It's the safest position you've been in since you've been in the field. We can see out for at least 1,000 meters below us, so we can see if they decide to attack from that direction. The men are dug in well and the mortar tube is ready. Our forward observer has the coordinates, so we can quickly call in artillery. It's as prepared as we can get."

"Yes, Sir. You're right. We can't get air support today, but maybe when the Spooky flies tonight it will slow 'em down a bit."

"I don't see why they haven't wiped us out yet."

"I can't figure it out, either. Since they have new equipment, I'm thinking they might be a very new unit. Probably very young soldiers. Or maybe they are just concentrating on a bigger plan and we're not worth the trouble. I just can't figure it out."

After working feverishly to get dug in, the men had some time to themselves before darkness fell. Men posted near the jungle side of the perimeter had seen several NVA walking along a trail at the edge of the jungle. They obviously had paths they frequently used. For some reason, they seemed totally unaware they were within range of Charlie Company. Twice since they'd been here a lone NVA soldier popped out of the jungle. Each time a rifle rang out putting an end to his duties. A man from the second platoon darted to the NVA, secured his weapon, and dragged him out of the path into the dense jungle foliage.

Fabe was enjoying his last cigarette. When they dropped off rations tomorrow morning, he would get more. He had only two cans of rations left. One he would eat tonight, and save the other one for the morning. His water was gone. "Damn, I'm thirsty. The stream ain't that far away."

Brian was sitting next to Fabe while Mex was keeping watch. "You know Merdis told us not to go get water. Suck on a stone."

"That doesn't even help anymore."

"At least you might get some sleep tonight. You won't think about the water while you're sleeping. Before you know it, morning will be here and we'll have a fresh supply."

"I don't know how you can be so damned confident they'll make it in tomorrow. You always think everything will turn out honkey-dorey." Tonight it really annoyed Fabe that Brian was so cheery.

"Don't be so negative. There's a lot of open area here for the chopper. God will supply." Brian had spent the last half hour reading his Bible. "Maybe if you took out your Bible and read it, you'd have a better attitude."

Fabe had no answer. Brian was probably right.

As Fabe was going to take the last drag of his cigarette, it fell from his hands as a mortar round exploded. The mortar fell well to the south of Charlie Company. Everyone jumped in their foxholes and crouched low, trying to get as much cover as they could. Hawk saw the mortars were coming from a southwest direction. Since it was out of range for High Angle Hell, he immediately called for artillery support.

There was a pause after the second mortar round exploded. Hawk knew this meant the NVA were recalculating to make their next hit closer to their target. He hoped they were out of range. His intuition proved true as a third mortar round hit closer, but still missing his men. This was followed by two RPGs which landed just short of his foxhole.

Minutes later, the requested artillery strike came in. The first strike was right on target, causing a secondary explosion in the distance.

Hawk looked in disbelief. "We sure as hell had those coordinates right on. They must have had a helluva lot of ammo there to cause such a big explosion."

"Let's hope it discourages the NVA from attacking tonight." Major Close knew Hawk's quick response to the first mortar had probably saved their lives.

By 1945 hours the men in the mortar platoon were settling in for the night. Cooper was already dozing. Amos spent the last fading minutes of daylight writing to his fiancé.

Every day we get fired at, and everyday someone is wounded or killed. To make matters worse, now we are out of water. I hope tomorrow is quiet so we can get supplies in.

As Amos re-read what he had written, he wondered if he had said too much. He didn't want to make Judy worry about him, so he ended the day's notes with encouraging words.

Don't worry about some of the stuff I said about how bad it is. I'm doing fine. Besides, I'm too damn stubborn to die. I'm so glad Mort was transferred to Mortars. We are in the safest position in Charlie Company. Keep making those wedding plans – I'll be home before you know it.

At 2000 hours Amos took over watch. As his eyes stared into the black night, his mind wandered back to the first time he'd taken Judy on a date. He had known her for two years, but he was afraid to ask her out for fear she'd say no. Then, when they were both Juniors in high school, his friends talked him into asking her to the Junior Prom. She said yes. It turned out to be one of the best nights of his life. She was so beautiful. She wore a long apricot dress and her red hair was swept up in a beehive. He had rented a tux with a white jacket. He remembered talking to her dad when he picked Judy up. Her dad warned him that he would still be up when they got home. He expected to see her hair looking exactly as it did when she left the house. It was a wonderful evening. They danced every dance. He'd always remember the smell of her perfume when he held her body close to his. And when he took her home her dad flicked on their kitchen light so he'd know he was being watched. Good thing they had left the prom a little early and went parking. There was a back road two miles out of town where they had spent the last half hour making out. He knew then she was the girl for him. In a month he would again enjoy the taste of her sweet kiss.

Dan took the next watch. He was talking to Deadeye, who was on guard duty in the next foxhole. "I got a letter from Ma when we were on Professional. She sent a clipping from the Benton Gazette. There was a fire in the kitchen at Lucy's Diner. Don't your sister work there?"

"Ya. Did it burn down?"

"Na. Just a grease fire, I guess."

"Wouldn't one of those cheeseburgers from Lucy's taste good right now?"

Dan let out a sigh. "You becha. With a cherry phosphate. My mouth's waterin' just thinkin' 'bout it."

"We're about outta food and water and the sons o'

bitches at home are eatin' cheeseburgers and drinkin' cherry phosphates. It ain't fair."

"You can say that again."

"In a couple of months we'll be heading back to the world. No more C rations. We'll get real food."

"This might be our last time in the field. I think we're due to be sent to the rear for the remainder."

"You might be right, Dan. They usually put you there the last month or two. I guess they figure if you survive that long, you deserve it."

"Amos is short, with only a month left, and he's still out here in the field."

"It's not right. He's earned time in the rear."

Dan and Deadeye had been silent for half an hour. Deadeye jumped when Dan started talking again. "You know what day it is?"

"Hell no. I think it was a Monday when we were dropped here."

"No. I mean, the day. Is it March sixth or seventh?"

"What the hell difference does it make? Is one day better than the other to die?"

"The seventh is my birthday."

"No shit! I think we got here on the third. I don't even know how many days we've been out here."

"Let's see. The first night we had no cover. The second night was back in the same place, only we dug in. Last night it rained."

"That means tomorrow's your birthday. We'll have a fuckin' birthday party!"

"What are we going to have at the party? Booze and girls?"

"Water and dinks."

"If we get water, that will be something to celebrate. I don't want any dinks at my party unless they're dead ones."

Brooklyn took over watch at 2200 hours while Deadeye and Chief tried to sleep. He was keeping a journal to record his time in Vietnam. Since he didn't have a chance to write in his journal today, he was reviewing the events in his mind so he wouldn't forget what he wanted to enter tomorrow. There was a lot to write. They had been hounded by the NVA all day and had taken several casualties, plus one more KIA. At least they were able to get them out. Then they had the feat of crossing the dike. It was amazing they all made it across. He would also make a note of their lack of water and food. He still had one can of food and some cheese and crackers in his rucksack. He would save the cheese and crackers as long as he could. He had a feeling it might be a while before they dropped supplies. There were so many NVA. They popped out everywhere. It was quiet now. Could it be the calm before the storm? His eyes strained to see any movement near or far. He hoped it would stay quiet so he could get some sleep tonight.

Lil' Bro sat in his foxhole. He knew he should be sleeping when he had a chance, but his mind wouldn't shut down. Although they were dug in deep, they were surrounded on three sides. They hadn't seen any NVA on the hill, but they must be watching the area. He looked at Merdis. He was damn lucky to get assigned to this company. Although they were on a horrific mission, these guys were unbelievable. He had heard rumors that some units did drugs and fought with each other. But he had seen none of that. In fact, when he first joined them, Merdis and Clark had approached him and warned him not to do drugs. Apparently, they had a talk with every new guy. "We don't do drugs here. We need every man, and we're not going to jeopardize anyone's safety because you're high." And that's how it was. Everyone looked out for each other. No drugs, no fighting among the men. Everyone watching each other's back. Like brothers.

He looked at Doc Bauer. He was finally sleeping. Lil' Bro had lost count of how many were wounded. And how many dead? Seven? Eight? It was way too many. No wonder it was taking a toll on Doc.

Lil' Bro got up and stood beside Merdis. He watched the Spooky approach and saw the first red curtain of fire rain down. "The first night the Spooky was terrifying. Now the roar is soothing to me. In fact, I can actually sleep better hearing it in the background. The silence is almost unbearable after it's gone."

"It's a sound you'll never forget. That, and the sound of a chopper coming in."

"There's a lot I'll never forget. Jumping into the rice paddy while I'm being shot at. The moaning of the wounded at night. The smell of the bodies we carried around. Longing for a simple thing like water."

"Your life'll never be the same."

Lil' Bro fought back tears as he thought of his life in Kansas. He knew he had changed already. He prayed that his wife would be able to accept that.

Six feet away, Fabe and Brian sat slouched against the wall of their foxhole. Fabe could hear Brian breathing, but it was too dark in the hole to see him. He could tell he wasn't asleep yet.

"I still think we could get to the stream and get some water."

Brian chuckled. "You need to think about something else. Besides, we're not going to have to go out there. They'll bring water tomorrow. You'll see."

"Did you ever watch Gomer Pyle on TV?"

"Sure. Didn't everybody?"

"You remind me of him. He always thought things would work out."

"I loved that show. And, as I recall, things always did work out ok."

"Ya, but it was kinda stupid. I mean, he wouldn't have lasted three days in the real Marines."

"It was one of my favorite shows. Gomer sure could sing good. I loved to watch Candid Camera, too. What TV show did you like?"

"I don't know. Laugh-In, Green Acres, Gunsmoke, the Smothers Brothers."

"All I remember about the Smothers Brothers is Tommy saying, 'Mom always liked you best'."

"I remember a show when they sang a song about draft dodgers. I thought it was funny at the time."

"Did you ever think of going to Canada?"

"Na. I mean, I talked smart. But I never really considered it. My brothers were in the military. One in Army, one in the Airforce. I just accepted that it was my turn. What about you?"

"I never even considered it. I didn't know you had brothers. You never told me about 'em."

"You never asked. They're a lot older than me. Like seventeen years older. One was killed in a car accident a week after he got out of the service."

"That's awful. Imagine surviving Nam and then getting killed when you get home."

"I was only six, so I guess I never thought about it that way. It would really be a bummer."

"Have you heard from your girlfriend lately?"

"Not my girlfriend anymore. She ditched me."

"I didn't know that."

"Good riddance."

Fabe didn't want to tell Brian that his girlfriend was dating his best friend. It still hurt too much to talk about it. "I still say we could get to the water."

"At home I used to let the water run until it got cold. I let it run down the drain."

"Me, too. And I used to let the water get nice and hot before I took a shower. Now I'd give anything for a shower – who cares if the water's cold?"

"I'll never waste water again."

"Me either."

Major Close sat on the floor of his foxhole next to Captain Hawk. "What's the deal with the scarfs your men are wearing? Everyone seems to be real proud of 'em."

"Yes, Sir. I had them made in a village near Chu Lai, north of the 198th Brigade. Everyone sneaks out to buy gum there. The supply sergeant has a girlfriend who's a seamstress. So, I commissioned her to make these scarfs. The black cotton is the same material the Vietnamese use to make their black pajamas. I wanted the men in Charlie Company to feel our unity, so I had her add a red "C" in the corner of the scarf."

"What on earth made you decide to do that?"

"We needed a morale booster. Our company gets sent to tough places. We're involved in lots of fights. We don't abuse the bad guys — which is a good thing. It seems like our men are always getting wounded. That can make them a little bit ornery."

"Of course."

"Well, one day the point man had shot a Vietnamese soldier. By the time I got up to the front of the line, they had propped the guy up with a cigarette burning in his mouth. It was kinda funny at the time, but then I thought about it. They had never done anything like that, and I was worried that it may be a precursor to doing something worse. I thought the scarf might help. When I gave it to them, I told them they should either wear it around their necks, keep it in their pocket to clean their weapon, or use it as a handkerchief. I also told them if they felt the need to do something to the dead gooks, they could leave a scarf as a sign we'd been there. As you can see, most of them wear it around their necks."

"It was a great idea to give each man a Charlie Scarf. You have a remarkable company of men."

"I think so, too."

The pilot of the Spooky knew he was limited where he could fly. He needed to be careful not to go too close to Alpha, Bravo, or Charlie Company. They had suffered heavy casualties already, and he wanted to be sure no one was wounded or killed in friendly fire. In less than two hours of pounding the area the Spooky flew off into the horizon.

CHAPTER 12

A Pathetic Sight

7 March 1969 – 0700 Hours

"Well, we survived another night." Captain Hawk surveyed the area assessing the damage done by the Spooky.

Major Close was disappointed. "I thought they would hammer the area for most of the night."

"With Alpha, Bravo, and us out here, they were limited where they could strike."

"It should slow down the NVA, anyway."

"Maybe. They have a way of surviving."

"As long as we can get in supplies today I guess they accomplished their mission."

The men who had rations left ate them for breakfast. The men who didn't glowered at those who had something to eat. JR was one of the latter. Chief was sitting next to him eating his last can of C rations.

"You're lucky you got somethin' left to eat."

Chief handed the can of teenie weenies to JR. "There's a few left. You can have 'em."

"Are you kiddin' me?" JR couldn't remember ever being so excited about rations.

Chief looked around at the other men. "What a pathetic sight we are. Look at Doc."

Doc Bauer was sitting with his head hung down. Blood had dried on his shirt and pants. His hair was filthy. His eyes looked tired and sunken in. He looked utterly defeated.

JR let out a sigh. "He sure has been busy. I couldn't even count the number of times we yelled 'medic!' in the last four days."

"I hope he's thinking about the lives he saved, and not the men who died."

"Me, too. When I first got here I thought the medics had it made. They never had to walk point. They travelled in the middle of the platoons where it was the safest. When we were in battle, they never had to go to the front."

Chief nodded in agreement. "I guess everyone thinks that at first. I actually thought they were cowards because most of 'em refused to carry a gun."

"After watching Doc, I think it's about the worst job you could have."

"I agree. I can't tell you how many times I've seen Doc run into the line of fire to help someone. Now I think medics are the bravest men here. I've seen Doc risk his life many times in order to save someone else."

"The poor bastard's run himself ragged."

Lil' Bro joined Fabe sitting on the edge of his foxhole. Fabe smiled as Lil' Bro opened his last can of food. "I see you did bring your ham and muthas'."

"Yup. I never thought I'd really eat 'em."

"You must be desperate."

"I'm so hungry I could eat the south end of a north-bound bear."

"Didja get any sleep last night?"

"A little. It's hard to sleep sitting up in a foxhole. You get all cramped up."

"If it's quiet tonight I'm gonna blow up my air mattress and sleep outside the foxhole."

"I think some of the guys did that last night. I thought about it. I just feel safer in the hole."

"It's not that much safer. If you stick close to the hole, you can jump in if any gunfire breaks out."

"Man, that sounds good. That's what I'm gonna do."

"Don't get your hopes up too high. You'll be more comfortable, but you still won't be able to really sleep. Not out here where we know we're surrounded."

At 1000 hours Captain Hawk put down the radio handset. "TOC said they would attempt to bring in supplies today. If they see NVA presence they will turn back. They've lost too many choppers already. Their priority is to save the choppers for evacuating men who are critically wounded."

"Look! Major Close pointed to the area they had seen the groups of NVA marching yesterday. "They're at it again."

"My God! After the Spooky made its rounds last night, I thought they'd be gone. I can't believe my eyes."

"How many do you think are out there?"

"I think there must be thousands of 'em. No matter what we do, they keep coming back. They're everywhere!"

"I guess that means no supplies today."

"I guess not."

Since the morning had been quiet, the men not on watch were moving from foxhole to foxhole to chat with the other guys. They were restless. Restless. Hungry. Thirsty. Tired. And scared.

Cooper was stretched out on the ground next to Deadeye and Dan. "It sure feels good to be able to lay down and stretch out."

"Yup. There's not much room in our foxholes."

"You can say that again."

"Let's see the picture of your girlfriend. JR told me she's a sight for sore eyes."

Cooper ran his fingers through his hair. "She's not my girlfriend. Just a girl I know. She's written to me, that's all."

Cooper's blue eyes sparkled when he brought out the picture of Peggy.

Dan's eyes flicked from the picture to Cooper and back again. "She's a dream. How'd you ever hook up with a girl like that?"

"She grew up in the house next door."

Deadeye snorted. "It's not fair. The girl that grew up next to me was a ditzy skank."

"And Peggy's a hellava nice girl. I've already got three letters from her."

Dan handed the picture back to Cooper. "It's better if she's not your girlfriend. Maybe then she'll keep writing to you."

"What's that supposed to mean?"

"Don't pay any attention to Dan. He's sore because he got a Dear John letter from Susie."

"Oh. That hurts."

"You wanna know what she said? Dear Dan, too bad you went off to risk your life in the fuckin' war. I'm busy screwing around with all the guys in town. Toodle-oo."

"Did she really say that?"

Dan couldn't believe Cooper was so naive. "No. But she might as well have."

"What about you, Deadeye? You got a girl?"

"Nah. Who'd want an ugly bastard like me?"

Cooper laughed. Deadeye was anything but ugly. In fact, he thought Deadeye might have had quite a few girls chasing after him.

"We better go take over watch so Amos and Mort can have a break."

"Ya sure know how to spoil a good time."

As Deadeye got up, he remembered. "Happy birthday, Dan!"

Cooper stared at Dan. "Today's your birthday?

Happy Birthday to you
You can suck on bamboo.
You smell worse than a dumpster,
And you look like hell, too."

"Thanks a lot."

"Aw, you know I don't mean anything by it. Are ya nineteen now?"

"Nope. I'm twenty."

Deadeye chuckled. "When we get sent back, we'll celebrate. I'll buy you a beer."

"Back where? To the rear or to the world?"

"The rear. Not the world — there you have to be twenty-one to drink."

"Funny, isn't it? I'm not old enough to drink in Arkansas. Not old enough to vote. But I'm old enough to fight in a war. Even die in a war."

Amos and Mort sat down by some scrub brush. Mort picked up a stone to suck on. "I don't know how long they expect us to stay out here with no food or water."

"Y'all gotta quit thinkin' about it. Let's talk about somethin' else."

"Ok. What do you want to talk about?"

"Judy."

"Geez. That's all you ever want to talk about."

"Did I tell you about her sister? Y'all will meet her at the wedding."

"What about her sister?"

"Her sister, Donna, is five-seven. She has dark hair and brown eyes. I'd say she's 36-24-36."'

"Keep talkin'."

"She loves soldier boys. And actors. You're gonna get lucky with her."

"You're full of shit. She's probably as ugly as a dog."

Amos laughed. "It's gonna be perfect. Me 'n Judy. You and Donna."

It was past noon when Clark and Merdis left Captain Hawk. Since no supplies were coming, they talked about ways to help their men cope. Hawk suggested they cut some bamboo that was on the edge of the jungle and take it back for the men. They could chop it open and get a little water from it. Merdis and Clark made their way over to the second platoon. As they squatted down and talked to one of the squad leaders, they kept their eyes on the nearby jungle.

"What the hell?" Clark couldn't believe what he was seeing.

Everyone around him stared at the sight at the edge of the jungle. A Vietnamese soldier was trying to sneak past them holding banana leaves in front of him. He was walking sideways.

Clark raised his M14 and put an end to the charade. "Did the mother-fucker think we wouldn't see him?"

"That dumb-ass! No wonder the dinks are losing the war."

As a couple of men from the second platoon went over to retrieve the dead soldier's weapon, Clark and Merdis followed them to the edge of the jungle.

Merdis had his machete out. "Y'all keep us covered while we cut some bamboo."

Merdis and Clark cut as many large stalks of bamboo as they could carry. They dropped some off by Captain Hawk and took the rest back to the third platoon. If the men used their machete to chop each section open, there would be a little water in most of the sections. It wasn't much, but it would be something.

Fabe picked the smallest piece of bamboo he could find from the pile and took it over to Lil' Bro. "Cut out a chunk of the outer layer and suck on it. It's good and moist. It'll help your thirst."

"Why didn't we get some sooner?" Lil' Bro grabbed the bamboo from Fabe. In excitement to appease his thirst, he grabbed his knife and gouged out part of the outer layer. He sucked on a chunk hoping to get some moisture into his mouth. His eyes bugged out. He coughed and spit it out. "What the fuck?"

Fabe doubled up laughing. Brian took out his camera and took a picture. Mex had tears running down his cheek.

"It's not funny! You bastards! Put that stupid camera

away." Lil' Bro threw down the bamboo and turned to walk away.

"Hey, don't be mad." Fabe grabbed Lil' Bro's arm to stop him. "The bamboo really does help your thirst." Fabe held up a large stalk of bamboo he brought along.

"Ya. Right. It's as bitter as hell, and you know it."

Mex smiled. He found it hard to keep from laughing again. "Only if you're dumb enough to suck on the stalk. There is actually water in it if you do it right."

Mex took the bamboo stalk from Fabe and gouged a large hole in the middle of a section with his machete. He took his cup from the bottom of his canteen, and he turned the stalk to let the water from the bamboo trickle out into the cup. He held it up. "Look. Water."

Fabe grabbed another stalk to do the same. "It's not much, but it wets your tongue. Just be sure you sip it first. Sometimes it's good, and sometimes it's bitter."

Lil' Bro grabbed a stalk to try getting some water out. He needed something to get rid of the bitter taste in his mouth. "You mean every section of the bamboo has some water in it?"

"No. That's the problem. It's a lot of work and you don't know if there will be water in there or not. And if there is water, it's not much."

Lil' Bro returned to his foxhole. He was writing a letter to his wife when Fabe and Mex brought the bamboo. He picked up the letter and read what he had written so far.

Cindy,

I am missing you and our son so much. I don't know why I let my parents talk me out of getting a deferment. I know I told you in previous letters that things weren't so bad. Well, that has changed. On Monday, we were dropped off in a rice paddy where we were being shot at as we landed. And it only went downhill from there. It was the worst day of my life. Things have not gotten any better, either. Men are being killed and wounded every day. The NVA are constantly assaulting us, and I see no let up in sight.

I am absolutely miserable. The temperature is at least 100 degrees. We're out of food and water. I have dried mud and blood all over my clothes. My feet are still damp from the rice paddy. There are mosquitoes and leeches constantly attacking us. I am so scared. I wonder if I'll ever make it. If there is a hell, this is surely it.

He picked up his pen and continued on.

Fortunately, I have met some great guys. I told you about Fabe. He's been looking out for me. Sometimes he gives me a rough time, but I know he always has my back. I couldn't ask for a better friend. All the men in our company are unbelievable. I have never seen a group of people where everyone is so totally committed to looking out for each other.

Lil' Bro dropped his pen when he heard the crack of the AK47. The men who were outside their foxhole dove for the closest foxhole when gunfire broke out from the jungle. The second platoon quickly took out the sniper.

Lil' Bro put away his pen and paper. He'd write more later. It was hard to concentrate when they were being shot at. Maybe sleeping outside the foxhole wasn't such a good idea, after all.

By late afternoon Brooklyn decided to eat the last of his food while there was no one nearby. He knew that no one else had food left, so he had to be secretive about it.

He jumped in his foxhole and dug the crackers and cheese out from the bottom of his rucksack. Then he pulled his poncho liner over his head so no one could see what he was doing. He jumped when he heard Rico's voice.

"Whatcha doin' in there? Why are you covered up?"

Brooklyn peeped his head out. "Damn it, Rico! Yuh scared the shit outta me."

"What are you doing in there, anyways?"

"Shaddup! Get in here if yuh wanna know, but doan make a scene."

Rico jumped in the hole and sat down. "Okay. Let's see why you're hiding."

Brooklyn whispered. "I got some crackas."

"Crackers? Where'd you get crackers?"

"I said, Shaddup! Do yuh want somebody tuh hear yuh?"

Rico whispered. "Where did you get the crackers?" "I been savin' 'em. If we stay in the hole, we can eat 'em and no one'll see us, okay? If anyone walks by we hafta be ready to hide 'em."

"Sure. Anything you say. Let's eat."

Brooklyn took out his P38 and opened the can labeled "crackers".

"Oh, my God!"

"Shaddup!"

"Sorry. I got a little excited. Let's eat."

"Not yet. I got some cheese, too." Brooklyn pulled out a small packet of processed cheese. He started to pull the poncho liner over them both.

Rico pulled it off. "For God's sake, hiding under a poncho liner only draws attention. Hell, that's what made me stop to see what you were doing."

Brooklyn took off his black C scarf and held it over the can so if anyone walked by they wouldn't see the food.

Rico took his knife and slit the package of processed cheese. Brooklyn carefully took out a cracker and squeezed some cheese on it. He popped it in his mouth.

He prepared the second cracker and gave it to Rico. Neither man said a word. They each had a second cracker with cheese. Brooklyn squeezed the last drop of cheese onto the last cracker. He broke it and gave half to Rico.

"My God, that was so good. I'm sure as hell glad I came along when I did."

At 1700 hours sniper fire broke out from the jungle. One of the men from the second platoon fired his M79 grenade launcher putting an end to the attack. They had encountered sniper fire earlier in the day with no casualties. This time one of the bullets put a hole in the arm of a man from the second platoon.

Captain Hawk could see the injury was not serious. He turned to Major Close. "I called TOC to get supplies and take out our wounded man."

"Do you think they'll come in for one guy who's not critical?"

"I told them our situation was getting desperate. They said they'd send a chopper."

Half an hour later a helicopter appeared on the horizon. Every man stopped and gawked at it, their mouth watering at the thought of a fresh supply of water.

The chopper remained high as it came closer. Enemy fire broke out. The chopper remained out of range as it disappeared into the horizon.

Captain Hawk turned to Major Close, "Why didn't they send a gunship? What the hell is going on at Brigade? They obviously have a bunch of inexperienced nincompoops running the place!"

"There must be a good reason."

"Why the hell didn't they leave you back there? At least they would've had someone who knows what they're doing."

"I appreciate your vote of confidence. It must be chaos there. New leaders and the 198th basically rendered helpless. I don't think I would have made any difference. Anyway, things always look different when you're sitting behind a desk."

CHAPTER 13

Desperate for Water

8 March 1969 – 0700 Hours

Merdis walked over to Captain Hawk. "I'm worried about Doc Bauer. You need to consider sending him back. I think he's having a nervous breakdown."

"Why? What happened?"

"Last night he sat hunched up all night with his head bowed, his arms wrapped around his knees. He was rocking back 'n forth and cryin'."

"Where is he now? I'll talk to him."

"He's still sittin' in the foxhole."

Hawk and Merdis walked back to the hole that held Doc Bauer. Captain Hawk jumped in and sat beside him. He could see Merdis was right. Doc never even looked up to acknowledge his visitor. "It's okay, Doc. You've done a remarkable job here. We'll take care of you."

Hawk joined Merdis who was waiting a few feet away. "I'll send him back as soon as we can get a chopper in. That poor guy's been through hell."

Mex just finished piling up several stalks of bamboo so it would be handy later while he was keeping watch. The bamboo didn't give much water, but right now it was keeping him going. He and Brian looked up to see what Clark's men were laughing about.

Clark saw that they were watching him and motioned for them to come over. "Hey, Brian, do ya know the difference between a smart Vietnamese soldier and a unicorn?"

"No. Tell me."

"Nothin'. They're both fictional characters."

Mex and Brian were glad for the diversion. Clark's jokes always decreased the tension.

"Ya got any more jokes?"

Clark paused to light a cigarette. He smiled at Brian and started chuckling even before he started telling his joke.

"A Sergeant was addressing a squad of eleven and said: "I have a nice easy job for the laziest man here. Put up your hand if you are the laziest."

Ten men raised their hands. The sergeant asked the other man, "Why didn't you put up your hand?"

The man said: "Too much trouble raising the hand, Sarge."

Mex returned an hour later to take over watch from Fabe. They usually didn't take turns watching during the day, as everyone was on high alert. But Merdis and Clark had asked their men to keep someone posted at all times. There were too many NVA around. They didn't want to take any chances of being caught off guard.

Mex turned to grab a piece of bamboo. It was gone. He looked at Fabe accusingly. "Who the hell stole my bamboo?"

"Don't look at me. I've been watching for the NVA. I didn't know I was supposed to guard your bamboo, too."

Brian looked around. There was no one else close by. "Don't blame Fabe. He's just doin' his job."

"Well, someone stole it." He looked accusingly at Fabe. "You were the only one here."

"I didn't take your stupid bamboo. Look around. No stalks here." Fabe smirked. "Maybe Lil' Bro didn't get enough yesterday, so he took it."

"It's not a joke. Taking someone's bamboo is serious business." Mex was pacing. "I'm gonna check with every son-of-a-bitch here. When I find out who it is, I'm gonna shoot the bastard."

"I think it's your time for you to take over watch. You're gonna havta let the thief live a little longer."

The sun was beating down on the men of Charlie Company. It was almost noon. Brian was on watch. Mex had given up on getting his bamboo back. He and Fabe were sitting on the edge of the foxhole, too hungry and thirsty to think of anything else. Fabe swallowed hard. "My mouth is drier than a popcorn fart in the month of July."

"I know. I can't even spit."

"I don't give a shit what anyone says, if we don't get water soon, I'm goin' out to that stream. It's not that far away." The more Fabe thought about it, the better it sounded.

"I'll go with ya. We'll either get shot, or we'll die of thirst. Right now, getting shot seems the better choice."

"Hell, yes! If we get wounded, we'll be taken out and sent home. We'll have plenty of water there.

"Or we'll be dead, and we won't know the difference."

"I think I might go to the next foxhole and pay a visit to Lil' Bro."

"You're gonna to ask him if he wants to go get water? With Merdis right there? He's never going to let us go out to the stream."

"You're right. I'll wait until Merdis leaves. He usually spends a lot of time with Clark. Hopefully, he'll head over by him soon."

"Do you really want Lil' Bro to come along with us?"

"I'm not askin' him to go along."

"Then why're ya gonna to talk to him?"

"When they dropped off the water a few days ago, Doc used it for the wounded. He must have an empty jug in his foxhole. Since he and Lil' Bro are in the same hole, I'm thinking I might be able to get my hands on a jug. We need a five-gallon jug to make it worth our effort."

"What about Doc? You think he'll cause any trouble?"

"Nah. This morning Lil' Bro told me he's crackin' up. I don't think he'll be a problem."

"You're serious about getting some water from the stream?"

"Yup. Are you really with me?"

"Damn right. If we have the jug and some canteens, it's worth a chance."

"That's what I'm thinking, too."

Fabe kept an eye on Lil' Bro and Merdis. He only had to wait a few minutes before Merdis walked over to Clark. Fabe took advantage and jumped in the hole beside Lil' Bro, who was on watch.

"Hey, Bro! How's it goin'?"

"Great... just great."

"What's your problem?"

"Oh, nothing. Life's great. I'm out here in this god-forsaken country. Hotter 'n hell. No food. No water. NVA creepin' around everywhere. Waitin' to get my head blown off. Listening to Doc freak out. I don't have a problem."

Doc was whimpering and rocking back and forth. "How long's he been like that?"

"All fuckin' night. I didn't get a wink of sleep."

Lil' Bro saw the smile on Fabe's face. "You think that's funny?"

"Hell, no. I just got other things on my mind."

"Like what? What makes you so cheery?"

Fabe didn't answer. He started shoving things around in Lil' Bro's foxhole. Doc paid no attention to him.

"What the hell you lookin' for?" Lil' Bro scowled as he watched Fabe.

"The empty five-gallon jug Doc had."

"It's under his rucksack. Why do ya want it?"

Fabe lifted Doc's rucksack and found the jug. He had a devilish grin on his face as he stood up.

"You ain't..."

"Shut up!" Fabe cut him off. "You better keep your trap shut. Just look the other way." Fabe leapt out of the foxhole and took his prize to show Mex.

"You son-of-a-bitch! You got it!"

"Yup. We have to plan this carefully and wait for the right moment."

Brian was listening, but since he was on watch, he had stayed out of it so far. He couldn't keep quiet any longer. "Don't you dare go without me. See if you can get one of the guys in the next foxhole to take over watch for me."

Fabe scampered over to the foxhole to his east. Willie, a self-proclaimed hillbilly, was sitting on the edge of his foxhole talking to Spinner. Both were from another squad in the third platoon. "What's up?"

"We need help. Three of us are gonna get some water from that stream. We need one of you to take watch for us."

Willie smiled, "It's about time someone had some guts. I've been trying to get these guys to go since yesterday, but they won't do it."

"Then you'll take Brian's watch?"

"Not me. I'm goin' along with you. Spinner can take watch."

Fabe, Mex, Brian, and Willie sat huddled together making plans. Brian would take his M60, so he could cover the others, if needed. Fabe, Mex, and Willie would leave their rifles behind, taking the five-gallon jug and as many canteens as they could carry. They would run between two other foxholes in a bit of a circuitous route to get to the stream, which was about 100 meters away.

Fabe took a deep breath. "It's been quiet all morning. I guess now is as good a time as any. Are you ready?"

"Let's do it!"

The four men crouched low and ran toward the stream carrying seventeen canteens and the five-gallon jug. The only weapon they brought along was Brian's M60, along with plenty of ammunition. When they got close to the stream Mex saw two large rocks. "Let's go behind the rocks!"

The men huddled behind rocks, deciding their next move. Brian would remain by the rocks to provide cover with his M60. He propped the '60 on the rock to steady it. "I'm ready when you are."

Mex looked at the stream. The stream was a little more than two meters wide, and fairly shallow. Somebody would have to step into the stream where it was deep enough to fill their containers. They would be out in the open. "I'll go first. When I get the jug filled, I'll hand it back to Fabe. He can give it to Willie who will bring it back by the rocks. Brian, you stay behind the rocks – you can't handle much with your M60 in your hands, anyway."

"Let's go!"

Mex, Fabe and Willie all ran to the edge of the stream. Fabe dropped his canteens and cupped his hands to drink some water. He splashed water on his face. Mex and Willie did the same.

"God, that's good!"

"Get going!" Brian was getting uneasy.

After another quick drink Mex stood with one foot in the stream. He squatted down to make himself a smaller target while he started filling the containers with water.

"What the hell's taking you so long? Fill those fuckin' canteens!" Brian was irritated that they had wasted time getting a drink, especially since he was stuck behind the rock. Now Mex was taking his good-natured time filling the canteens.

Mex looked up. "There's a lot of water bugs. I'm trying not to get so many in the canteen."

"To hell with the water bugs. Just fill the canteens. Who cares anyway? It's water!"

Fabe and Willie quickly filled two canteens each and rushed them back to Brian. By that time, Mex had filled three canteens. He handed them to Fabe. Fabe gave Mex the five-gallon jug. Then he gave the full canteens to Willie, who in turn sat them down next to the rock by Brian.

By this time, Merdis and Clark had spotted them. "Holy shit!"

"Those stupid fuckers!" Clark grabbed his rifle and ran toward the foxhole closest to the stream so he could give them cover, if needed. Merdis was right behind him.

Mex had just handed the five-gallon jug to Fabe, and was filling the eighth canteen when sniper fire broke out from across the stream. Willie fell to the ground. Fabe kept the jug in his hand as he rushed to Willie. Mex joined him and together they dragged Willie behind the rocks. Mex looked at Willie and saw red liquid saturating his pants by the back of his right knee. Brian stepped slightly to the left and frantically searched the horizon to see where the rifle fire was coming from. He sighted in on the sniper. Grasping the cocking handle, he pulled the trigger.

Click. The weapon misfired. His step to the left had left him partially exposed. "I'm hit!" Brian cried as he fell backward.

By now all the men of Charlie Company were watching, wondering what was going on. Those nearest the stream laid fire in the direction of the sniper. The sniper was out of their range, but hopefully it would discourage him.

Meanwhile, the men behind the rocks huddled together. They could hear the chink of the bullets hitting the rock. Willie frantically pulled up his right pant leg. Mex could see where the round had gone in one side of his knee and out the other. There was a hole two inches in size with a big chunk of meat hanging off. Mex took his C scarf off, wrapped it around Willie's knee, and tied it.

Fabe turned to Brian. He couldn't see any blood on him. "Where are you hit?"

"My leg." Brian grabbed at his left upper leg. It felt dry. "I don't know. There's no blood."

"Can you stand on it?"

Brian tested his left leg by slowly putting some weight on it. "Ya. I can stand."

"What happened to the '60?"

"Don't know. It just misfired. Jammed or something. I'll eject a few and try again. Let's pray it works this time."

Hawk ordered the mortar platoon to fire High Angle Hell. Before Brian got his rifle up they fired two rounds toward the sniper.

Fabe was surprised to see the explosion where the sniper had previously been. Grabbing the jug and canteens that were standing beside the rocks, Brian and Fabe scrambled to get back inside their perimeter. Willie put his arm around Mex and hobbled back. They didn't bother with the empty canteens.

Since Doc Bauer was out of commission, another medic ran to meet them along with Clark and Merdis. All was quiet. The medic tended to Willie's leg. He turned to Hawk who had joined them. "It's not life-threatening, but if he wants to keep his leg we need to get him outta here."

Merdis scowled at Fabe, Brian, and Mex. "What the hell were you thinking? You can't go out there without telling us. We could've mistaken you for the NVA and opened fire!"

"If we woulda told you, you woulda stopped us from going."

"Damned right, I woulda!"

Brian was still stunned. He wasn't really hurting, and he didn't know why he wasn't bleeding from the bullet that knocked him down. He reached in his left cargo pocket and felt his Kodak camera. He pulled it out. The bullet was embedded in his camera. "Holy shit! Will you look at this?"

Fabe stared at the camera. "That camera saved your sorry ass! You are one lucky son-of-a-bitch!"

"It has nothing to do with luck. My guardian angel was with me."

Clark lifted the five-gallon jug. There were several bullet holes in it. Only two inches of water remained in the jug. He passed the canteens to the men around him.

Fabe stepped away from Brian. "Hey! Give me some of that water!"

"Too late. It's already gone."

"Son-of-a-bitch! All that for nothin'."

Brian scowled. "At least you got a drink from the stream. I didn't get shit."

Mort and Dan were inspecting High Angle Hell, making sure it was ready to fire again, if needed. Mort tried to wet his lips with his tongue, but his tongue was too dry to do any good. "You'd think we would have gotten some of that water after we saved their asses."

"I heard the five-gallon jug was shot all to hell. I guess they only got back with a coupla canteens."

"We shoulda got one of 'em. It just ain't fair."

"Nothin's fair out here."

Hawk was shaken by the fact that his men were desperate enough to risk their lives for water. He had to do something. He needed to do it now. "I have to convince TOC they need to bring food and water. I'll make a plea when we call in for a dustoff to take Willie out."

Major Close nodded in agreement. "I'll call TOC. Maybe I can convince them."

Major Close was on the radio for several minutes. Hawk could see it took all his effort to keep himself under control. "I told them we have two wounded. I might have made their wounds sound worse than they are. I also said we had one guy that was delirious. Then I reminded them of the papers we got off the NVA officer. They said they will attempt sending a chopper with water, food, and ammo when they pick up the three men and the papers. They can't guarantee they'll make it in. They're coming from LZ Baldy.

"Why not Professional?"

"Professional has been taking too many hits from mortars."

"At least you convinced them to attempt a delivery and pickup."

"I did my darndest to make them understand how desperate the situation is."

"Thank you, Sir. I appreciate it."

Hawk was concerned that if the choppers did actually drop off water everyone would leave their post and rush to get it. It would leave a spectacular target for the NVA.

He picked up the radio handset. "All platoon leaders report to headquarters immediately."

In a few minutes everyone was assembled, including a few squad leaders. "Major Close has spoken to TOC. They're sending in a chopper to pick up the wounded and drop off supplies. I want three men from each platoon assigned to retrieve the supplies. One will be assigned to retrieve water, one to get rations, and one to retrieve ammunition. I want everything distributed evenly."

Amos wanted clarification. "What about medical supplies? My medic said they were short days ago."

"We requested 'em. The three remaining medics will be responsible for picking them up and dividing them equally."

"Amos, have the mortar tube and the recoilless ready. Anyone not assigned a specific job will provide security for the chopper."

Merdis spoke up. "I'll see that Doc Bauer gets on the chopper."

"Good. The medics will be responsible for getting the two wounded men on the chopper. It's your job to inform your men and assign their jobs. I don't want to see everyone in the company rushing out there when the chopper comes in. Be sure they understand exactly what they need to do. I'm holding each of you responsible for the actions of your men."

Forty-five minutes later two choppers appeared on the horizon. A gunship led the supply chopper into the area. As the gunship fired into the surrounding area, the men on the supply chopper pushed off water, rations, ammo, and medical supplies. Then they loaded Willie, the man wounded the day before, and Doc Bauer on the chopper. Hawk handed the pilot the papers they had taken off the NVA officer. The men cheered as the choppers lifted off.

Mort, Brooklyn, and Rico were assigned to get the supplies for their platoon. Before the choppers had started their ascent with the wounded, the three men were on their way to collect the goods. Without a word, they grabbed water, food, and ammo and ran back to the mortar platoon. The men waiting gave them a slap on the back when they returned safely.

Mort was holding two five-gallon water jugs. He handed one to Amos. The men quickly lined up. Mort and Amos poured a small amount in each man's canteen cup. Then Mort poured some in his own cup and took a drink of the precious liquid.

Once they had a taste of the water, Mort and Amos took their time filling up a canteen for each man.

The mood of the men in Charlie Company seemed more like men attending a party than a group of worn-out soldiers. The men took long swigs of water but were careful to save some for later. Then they had a feast on C rations.

Dan sat beside Deadeye. "Who thought a can of rations left over from 1952 would taste so damn good?"

"It's almost like Christmas!"

"Merry Christmas, good buddy!"

"No, it's Happy Birthday!"

Dan and Deadeye chinked their canteens together in a toast. "To many more!"

Dan smiled. "To many more, indeed."

"I can't believe the choppers made it in with the supplies and picked up the wounded without receiving any enemy fire."

Dan lit a cigarette and laid back. "Water, food, and cigarettes. What a great birthday — even if it is a day late."

"What more could you want?"

"Nothing. Except a helicopter to take us out of this hell-hole."

Deadeye's smile faded. "That's what we really need. I don't know how much longer we can stay trapped here. I hope we don't run out of food and water again."

"I don't see how we can stay here much longer. It looks to me like we're down almost half of our men."

"I'm guessing Alpha and Bravo aren't in any better shape than we are. Something has to happen soon."

CHAPTER 14

Advancing Up the Hill

1300 Hours

Captain Hawk sat on the edge of his foxhole. The NVA soldiers in the distance were still marching around. Nothing had changed there. But things sure had changed within his company. His men were all in good spirits. They were eating and drinking. Even laughing. Maybe it was a blessing that the men went for the water. Three made it out without a scratch. Only Willie got wounded. His injury wasn't life threatening, but it was bad enough to convince TOC to send in a chopper. *Willie will be ok. He'll be going home.* That's something everyone longed for.

It was Hawk's second tour of duty, but it didn't decrease his longing to go home. He wanted so badly to see his family. Being in charge, he couldn't let his men see how lonesome he was for his own wife and kids. He needed to portray the strong leader. In another month, he would go to Hawaii on R and R. Mary and the two kids would meet him there. John was five years old. Nancy was only a year old. John would be happy to see him, but he wondered if Nancy would even remember him. A month seemed like forever. They hadn't been in the field even a week and he'd seen so much death and destruction. He prayed the new commanding officer would see the odds they were up against. If he did, he would surely evacuate them or send in reinforcements. In reality, they probably didn't have any reinforcements to send in. If they wanted to evacuate the men, they would have already done it. At times like this he wondered why he had chosen a career in the military.

Major Close was sitting beside him. "It sure is quiet."

"It's quiet here, but there sure was a lot going on close

by this morning. I think it must be Alpha that's getting hit hard."

"I was expecting the same here. I can't believe that chopper came in, dropped off supplies, and took men out without receiving any enemy fire. That's too good to be true."

"Yes, Sir. You're absolutely right. I'm afraid it's the breath before the plunge. The NVA had a reason they let the chopper in. I hope it doesn't give TOC a false sense of security."

"Me, too." Major Close gave Hawk a lazy smile. "Whatever the reason is, I'm glad we got re-supplied. I'm mighty grateful for the food and water. It's the first time since I've been in the field that we've been able to really take a deep breath and recharge."

Fabe finished three cans of food — turkey loaf, ham slices, and fruit cocktail. He opened a can of pound cake and set the cake aside. He took out his "church key" to punch triangular holes in the bottom of the can for ventilation. Then he pried apart a claymore. It could only be detonated with a fuse, so it was safe to handle. He took out the chunk of C-4. The C-4 was a curved plastic block of explosive. The block was pliable, and he easily broke off a chunk a little smaller than a golf ball. He passed the block on to Mex. Heat tablets were included with their C rations, but it took a lot longer to warm anything with them. Fabe put the chunk of C-4 into the can and lit it with his Zippo lighter. He put water in his canteen cup and heated it before adding his instant coffee. It was the first coffee he'd had since he'd been in the field. He enjoyed it with the pound cake. Mex did the same.

Fabe relaxed for the first time since he'd been there. After finishing his pound cake he lit a cigarette. "This is more like it."

Mex smiled. "It sure is."

Fabe got out his billfold and marked another day off his

calendar. A day closer to going home. As he put the calendar back, his eyes fell on the money he had in there. Actually, he had no real money. In Vietnam they were only issued the Military Pay Certificates. The MPCs were similar to a dollar bill, but smaller. They came in denominations from five cents to twenty dollars. They couldn't use US dollars in Vietnam.

Fabe had most of his paycheck sent home where his parents would put it in a bank account for him. "I don't know what good it does to have these MPCs. They're only good in Vietnam, and we hardly ever get to the rear to spend 'em."

"I got a bunch of 'em, too. Maybe after this, they'll send us to the rear. I want to buy my wife a new stereo and have it sent home. They got some real good ones in the PX. They're a lot cheaper than they are back in the world. If you can't spend your MPCs, I'll be happy to help you."

"I bet you would. Anyhow, I send most of my money home, so it doesn't really amount to that much."

"Think of all the money you'll have in the bank when you get home."

"I woulda made twice as much as I get here. I had a good job in a foundry."

"But you probably woulda spent it. Now you'll have a nice pile of money in the bank."

"I 'spose. Same for you. What are you gonna do with your money when you get home?"

"I won't have any left. It all goes to my wife."

"Doesn't she have a job? I mean, what else would she do with her time?"

Mex smiled. Fabe obviously didn't understand women. "Sure, she has a good job. She's a nurse. But she's not a saver. She'll have it all spent on clothes, shoes, purses. And probably goin' out and partying."

"Bummer."

"What'll you do with your money, Fabe?"

"I don't know. Maybe I'll buy a new car."

"If I wasn't married, I'd get a Mustang. Seafoam green."

"Ya. That would be a chic magnet."

"Or maybe yellow. My wife really likes yellow cars."

"Have you seen the Firebirds? They've only been out a coupla years."

"I've seen 'em. That'd be a good choice. You could sure burn rubber with one of those."

"Maybe even a convertible."

"What color?"

"Red."

"The cops'll be after you all the time! A red sports car is like a bullseye to a cop."

Fabe smiled. "I could get a big engine and out run 'em."

"I bet you could, too."

Fabe's smile faded from his face. "We gotta get out of here first."

"We will, Fabe. We will."

It was 1440 hours when Major Close turned to Captain Hawk. He hung up his radio handset. Hawk could see by the look on his face that they weren't getting evacuated.

"Well, Hawk, this is the moment we've been dreading. Alpha got hammered with mortars this morning, like we thought. They took significant losses. They are desperate for us to get to them. Since the choppers made it in here without incident, TOC feels it's a good time for us to move out. They want us to proceed to meet up with Alpha Company ASAP. Bravo has also been taking heavy casualties. Right now, they are attempting to make their way to our current position. If all goes as planned, they should be here in less than two hours. They'll take over this area tonight. After we meet up with Alpha, they'll follow us. The plan is for us to all join up tomorrow."

"That means going up the hill. We've been sitting here, and we can see these clowns marching 1,000 meters away. They can see us walking around. They know we're here.

They're waiting for us to do something. If we move up that hill I'm afraid they're going to smoke us with mortars." Hawk wiped the sweat from his brow. "We only have seventy men left. We're gonna take casualties. Probably a lot of casualties."

"I won't disobey orders again. We gotta do it."

"Yes, Sir. Let's go."

Hawk met with his platoon and squad leaders. "We're gonna move out. We'll be advancing up the hill."

Clark looked at Hawk in surprise. "Sir, I'm afraid they may be waiting for us to do that."

"Alpha Company took heavy casualties this morning. We need to give them support."

Amos couldn't keep quiet. His gut told him it was a bad idea. "I agree with Clark. It's like walking into a death trap."

"Orders are orders. I have considered our options, and we will proceed. We're the infantry. Soldiers trained for combat. There will be no further discussion on this matter."

"Yes, Sir."

"Tell your men to be ready in fifteen. We'll fan out as we proceed up the hill. No point in making a big target for 'em. We'll head out in the order we're dug in. Mortars, first platoon, and headquarters will go up over the wall and stay in the middle. The third platoon will stay to the right, and the second platoon to the left. Amos, have your men ready to set up the mortar tube in the bomb crater halfway up the hill. I want you ready to fire by the time the rest of the men get to the top of the hill. Have the men carrying the recoilless ready, too."

"Yes, Sir."

Fabe, Mex, and Brian had been talking about their escapades of the morning when Merdis walked over to give them their orders.

Brian didn't look at Merdis. "I'm sorry we caused so much trouble this morning."

"It was a damned fool thing to do." His voice softened. "I'm just glad you three got back ok."

"We were desperate."

"I know. I understand why you did it. But it was a hell of a risk you were taking."

"We knew it was risky. We were willing to take our chances."

"Well, it's over now. You can stop flapping your jaws and get your shit together. Y'all got a war to fight."

"We're moving out?"

"Y'all be ready in ten. We'll be advancing up that hill. Either we'll join up with Alpha Company or we'll die tryin'."

"The Lord will take care of us like he did this morning."

Fabe scowled. "Like He took care of Sanchez and Cal?"

"I guess it was just their time."

"I sure as hell hope it's not our time."

"You have to look on the positive side. You know — the glass is half full, not half empty."

Fabe was fed up with Brian's refusal to face things the way they were. "Zip it up, Gomer. We don't all see things the way you do."

Fabe chugged his second cup of coffee and put his cup back on his canteen. "I guess the party's over."

Lil' Bro walked over to Fabe and handed him a letter that was ready to be mailed. Fabe looked at the envelope. It was addressed to "Mrs. Aloysius Brothers". "Why you givin' me this?"

Lil' Bro nervously looked off into the distance. "Fabe, you're the best friend I have. I need you to be sure this gets sent to my wife if I..."

"If you get killed? 'Cause if that's what you're going to say, it's crazy. Nothin's gonna happen to you."

"Fabe, please."

"Anyway, what makes you think I'm gonna make it?"

"I figure there's a good chance one of us'll make it. You

sure as hell know a lot more about survivin' out here than I do. Promise me."

"I promise." Fabe took the letter and put it in his rucksack. "But, in case you haven't noticed, the NVA don't distinguish between the cherries and the seasoned men. Look at Sanchez and CJ. Hell, they were as good as they get."

Lil' Bro turned to walk back to his foxhole to finish organizing his rucksack. He took three steps and stopped, turning back to Fabe. "Thanks."

Brian walked over to Fabe. "What was that all about?"

"Lil' Bro wrote his old lady a letter in case he don't make it."

Brian was silent.

"Damn it all, Brian! I'm so sick of this fuckin' war."

"You gotta put it out of your mind. That's the only way you'll get through this."

"I know. You're right. You, Mex, and Lil' Bro are my best friends here. You know I try not to get close too many guys. It's so much easier if you don't know 'em. We've lost so many already. When they're your good friends it's so much harder to keep goin' on."

"But we have to keep going. We have to keep focused to stay alive. God will help us."

"He sure helped you today."

"He sure did."

"Well, we're going to need all the help we can get. I'm afraid Lil' Bro has the right idea. I'm afraid the death toll will go up today."

"There you go again. Always thinking negative thoughts."

"I'm just facing the facts: The NVA has been watching us. We're down to half our size. We're heading up an open hill to get to Alpha, who is surrounded. What are our chances?"

"You're exaggerating. We're not down to half."

"Give it up, Gomer! You know we're headed for trouble."

"Quit calling me Gomer! I'm not stupid! I choose to look at the positive side of things. I don't need you or anybody else trying to make me see things differently. I refuse to think that evil will outdo good. Your cup may be half empty, but my cup is always full because God refills it. I know everything is in the Lord's hands." Brian turned and walked away.

As the mortar platoon was also getting ready to move out, Amos pulled out the picture of Judy. He looked at it one last time. "I love you," he whispered.

Amos didn't hear Mort walk up next to him. "I love you, too."

"What the hell you doin' spyin' on me?"

"I thought you were talkin' to me."

"You knew damn well I wasn't. If I was talking to you I'd have said to go fuck yourself."

Mort laughed. Leave it up to Amos to lighten his mood.

"Did you want something? Or did you just come over to tell me you love me?"

Mort got serious. "I was wondering what you thought about heading up that hill."

"I think it's a piss poor idea. I think the NVA are waiting for us to make that move."

"I got a real bad feeling about this."

"Me, too. But we don't really have a choice, do we?" Amos put his picture away.

"Maybe you should go talk to the captain about it. He might listen to you."

"We already talked about it at our meeting. It's a done deal."

"I was afraid of that."

"Mort, gimme the baseplate. It doesn't pay for you to strap it to your rucksack. I need to get the mortar tube set up right away, anyhow. You concentrate on covering our backs."

Chief and Deadeye had cleaned and checked over the recoilless. "I guess we're as ready as we'll ever be."

"Guess so."

Dan was standing next to Deadeye. "It's gonna get rough today."

"Look at it this way: It's one day closer to going home. Like I said yesterday, this could be our last mission in the field. We've lost so many men that it'll take a while to rebuild our company. By then, they might have us stationed in the rear."

"God, I hope so."

"I won't know what to do first when I get back to the world. Maybe just stand in the shower for a long time. Or drink some nice cold water. Or go down to Lucy's for that cheeseburger and cherry phosphate".

Dan gave an evil grin. "I know what I'm gonna do. I'm gonna look up Susie and tell the cheating bitch to go to hell. And kiss my ass on her way down."

The men were strung out in a jagged line as they began their ascent up the hill. The hill wasn't very steep. Climbing the hill wasn't the problem. The problem was what was on the other side of the hill.

The third platoon, being on the right, passed a few old foxholes. Fabe was the last man on the right side of the company. He loosened his grip on his rifle. He'd been holding on so tight that his knuckles were white. Trying to keep calm, he took a deep breath. Brian was walking to his left. His lips were moving, and he looked like he was in another world. Fabe knew he was talking to God. Maybe praying. Maybe pleading. Maybe making God a deal if he spares his life.

Fabe looked beyond Brian to where Lil' Bro was keeping pace with Merdis. They were slightly ahead of the group. Lil' Bro swept his left hand across his face to get rid of the sweat running down. Fabe forced his shaking legs to keep moving. Since he was at the end of the line, he scanned the brush and grass which cropped up about twenty meters to his right. He felt eyes watching him. He couldn't see movement or any sign of NVA in the scrub brush. He looked behind – there was nothing there. He wanted to run or hide. There was no place to go. Nowhere to run to. Nothing to hide behind. His fear mounted with every step.

In the center of the group, the mortar platoon was making their way uphill. Mort was walking to the left of the crater. He looked carefully for any signs of booby traps. The hill was a good place for the NVA to plant land mines. There was nothing to indicate any kind of trap. Amos and Rico were to his right, inside the crater. They also had their eyes down, searching the ground for any indication of mines. Deadeye, Dan, and Chief were in the middle of the crater.

Amos ran ahead to the center of the crater to set up High Angle Hell, as ordered. Deadeye hustled to give him a hand. He sat down his rucksack and his rounds for the recoilless before getting out his entrenching tool. Walking over to Amos, he began levelling the area for the mortar tube.

Amos was already starting to assemble High Angle Hell, along with Rico. "The ground here is soft and pretty flat. It won't take much to make it level."

Mort started toward the crater to give them cover while they were setting up the mortar tube. Everything was so quiet he could hear his heart beating. His breath was keeping time with the song playing inside his head. *We've gotta get out of this place, if it's the last thing we ever do.*

The silence was broken when the men heard the THOOP, THOOP, THOOP of mortars being dropped into tubes and coming out. The screeching – SSSSSS, like a sizzling sound, followed.

"INCOMING!"

"INCOMING!"

"INCOMING!"

CHAPTER 15

Incoming

1515 Hours

The men in Charlie Company turned to retreat and ran like hell. Captain Hawk was walking five meters to the left of Mort, and slightly ahead of him. Instinctively, he headed for the bomb crater as his heart hammered in his chest. He had taken only four steps when his FO grabbed his leg. "Hawk! Get in here! Get down!"

Hawk turned to jump into one of the abandoned foxholes with his FO, but could see that there was no room for him. His RTO had already jumped in. As Hawk turned back to head for the bomb crater, he spotted another foxhole. It was much closer than the crater. As he jumped in and crouched down, a mortar exploded behind him, sending chunks of earth flying in all directions. This was exactly what he had been dreading.

Major Close followed Hawk into the foxhole, landing beside him just as the mortar hit the ground. He wished he hadn't been sent into the field. What good had it done? He might have done more good back at TOC. Maybe he could have convinced someone there that this was a bad move. But probably not. The ground shook as another mortar landed close by. He held his breath and closed his eyes in dreadful anticipation of where the next mortar would land.

The third platoon was scrambling for any cover they could find. Fabe turned and ran back in the direction he came from. He didn't see a foxhole close by, so he headed toward the scrub brush. Before he got to the brush, he spotted a dark area in the ground. When he got a couple of steps closer, he could see it was a trench. He couldn't believe his luck. He hadn't seen the trench on his way up the hill. It was about four feet deep and eighteen inches wide. He noticed that it went in a zig-zag fashion for quite a distance. At this point the trench was running perpendicular with the hill. Jumping in the trench, he crouched down, grasping his rifle in front of him. Each time he heard the thoop of a mortar he jumped. He knew that he was pretty safe in the trench unless the mortar was a direct hit. Then it would be deadly. The screeching whistle that lasted less than five seconds left him frozen with terror as he helplessly waited, praying it would miss him.

Merdis, Brian, and Mex ran toward a foxhole a couple of meters away. Merdis reached it first. As he landed in the hole, he instinctively looked down to check for any booby traps. His eyes grew big as he saw three prongs sticking out of the ground. Too late. He was already in the hole, his knee just inches from the prongs. His momentum forced him to land on his knees and hands. Knees straddling the prongs, he sucked in his breath. He stiffened his arms to support his body. No sooner than he had seen the Bouncing Betty when the thump of Brian's body landed on top of him. In a spasm of panic, he struggled to remain on his hands and knees, keeping his back arched. His eyes were glued to the three prongs below him. "GET OFF!"

Another thump as Mex landed on top of Brian. "Get down!"

"Get the fuck off!" Merdis didn't know how long he could keep from collapsing with two people on top of him. He held his breath and his heart pounded like a jackhammer.

"Get down!" Mex was exposed as mortars were landing around him. Why the hell didn't the other guys get down?

"GET OFF! MINE!" Merdis' words were drowned by the explosion nearby.

Brian was starting to panic. "GET DOWN!"

"BOUNCING BETTY! GET THE FUCK OFF!"

Brian only heard the word *Betty.* His stomach turned to ice as he shouted to Mex. "GET OFF! BOUNCING BETTY!"

The color drained from his face as Mex scrambled out of the hole. He couldn't get his hands and feet to move fast enough. He stood beside the foxhole paralyzed. Where should he go?

Brian let out a sigh of relief as he felt the weight lifted off his back. Not daring to breathe until he was out of the hole, he quickly joined Mex. He grabbed Mex's arm and turned to run for the crater. "NO!" Mex pointed to a foxhole only a few meters away. Brian followed his lead and jumped into the foxhole beside him. He held his breath, hoping this hole didn't have a land mine in it.

Merdis was still huddled over the Bouncing Betty. His muscles seemed incapable of moving. He was focused on the three prongs; he barely noticed the thump of the mortars around him. Breathing through his nostrils to control his jagged breaths, he clenched his teeth. Never taking his eyes off the Bouncing Betty, he slowly forced himself to lean backward and put his weight onto his feet. On shaking legs he stood up, then crawled out of the foxhole. He ran to find another foxhole as fear trickled down his spine. As he was about to dive into it, he stopped short. This time he would look where he was going. Scanning the bottom of the foxhole, he could see no signs of a booby trap. He let out a sigh of relief as he jumped in for cover.

Lil' Bro had seen Merdis, Brian, and Mex pile into a foxhole. Knowing there would be no room for him in there, he frantically looked around to see where everyone was headed. He spotted Fabe running toward the scrub brush to the east. Taking off in a run, he was almost caught up to Fabe when he disappeared from sight. Lil' Bro stopped dead in his tracks. How could Fabe just vanish? Then he saw the trench only two meters in front of him, running parallel to the hill. That must be where Fabe went. He covered the distance in two steps. Diving into the trench head first, he flattened himself out. "Oooooff!"

He felt like a ton of bricks landed on top of him as the air was knocked out of his lungs. He opened his mouth and gasped for air like a fish out of water. Had he been hit? Did the trench cave in on top of him? Slowly air started filling his lungs. The pain in his chest subsided. He lay still, recovering his breath. Now he could see that the trench had not caved in. As he tried to roll over to see what happened, his rucksack and radio blocked the way. Then he realized that the heavy load on his back knocked the wind out of him when he landed in the trench. *Thank God!* He lay flat on his stomach, forcing his breathing to return to normal.

Mort was heading for the bomb crater to join Amos, Deadeye, Chief, and Rico. When the sizzling whistle of the mortar announced it's coming, they all dropped to the ground where they stood.

Mort wished he was in the bomb crater. He was lying face down on the ground with no cover whatsoever. His nose dug into the dirt. Opening his eyes, he saw an ant crawling. His world focused on that tiny ant. It was so very small. The ant quickly disappeared into the safety of its hole. Mort wished he were that ant. Did the ant realize how lucky he was that he could crawl into the hole and disappear? If only Mort had somewhere to disappear to. He blinked. There was nowhere to go. No way to escape.

Mort listened to the screech of the mortars as they left the tube. While the sound of an incoming mortar is easily identified, there is no way of predicting where the mortar will fall. It could be on top of you, next to you, or fifty meters away.

Mortar rounds were dropping all around him. He turned his head to see what was happening to his left. JR was lying in a prone position eight feet away, where he had been walking up the hill. Mort flinched when he saw a round land four feet on the other side of JR. All Mort could see was the top of his helmet. There was no way of knowing how severely JR was injured. Or if he was alive. He watched for movement.

JR had been headed for the bomb crater but knew he couldn't make it before the round landed. He fell face down on the ground and laid as flat as he could. As the mortar exploded nearby, he could feel nothing but blind terror. He felt pressure as pieces of shrapnel and dirt sprayed his helmet. He jerked back his hands. It felt like there were needles piercing them under his nail beds. Coughing from the dust and smoke, he fought to get some air into his lungs. Lifting his head, he turned to the right. As the dust filtered away, he saw Mort staring at him.

"You're alive! I thought you were dead."

"So did I!"

"Boy, am I happy to see your face!"

Weighed down by dread, JR struggled to lift his arm to feel for blood. He touched the back of his neck and felt the warm sticky fluid. He could move his head ok, and he couldn't feel any open wounds. Managing to raise his left arm higher, he felt his helmet. The outside canvas was shredded. The metal pot underneath was rough and pitted in where it had been pelted by debris. It was still intact. He lowered his hand and studied it. He looked unbelievingly at the dirt painfully embedded under his fingernails. How was it possible that he was still alive?

Mort continued to lie flat as mortar rounds landed all round him. Each time he heard a mortar leave the tube, he shut his eyes in dread. His hands were clenched on both sides of his helmet. Suddenly, he felt an adrenaline surge. He couldn't stay still. Wanting to know what was happening, he raised his head and looked toward the crater. A mortar landed between him and Amos, blocking his vision with dust and dirt from the explosion.

Men were screaming in pain. "MEDIC!" "MEDIC!"

Some were screaming for help for themselves, some for others.

The screaming was coming from the men in the crater. Mort looked in that direction. That's where Amos had been. Before he could focus on anyone, another round exploded. The impact threw him back a couple of feet. He landed on his back. The color drained from his face as it went slack. He stared wide-eyed at the sky, seeing nothing. His breath was coming in shallow waves. Although it was only a moment, time stood still for Mort. His heart slammed against his chest with each beat.

Slowly, his eyes began to focus on the smoke-filled sky. Gulping for air, he felt reality resurrecting. Letting out a sigh, he tried to lift his head. If felt as heavy as an anvil. He took deep breaths as he tried to clear his thoughts. *What happened? Where am I?* Lying motionless, he tried to make sense of it all.

A loud "thoop" made him realize he was in the middle of a war. His senses returned. He felt warm liquid running down his left arm. There was no pain. Dizziness threatened to overtake him as he struggled to raise his head. He saw the blood on his left upper arm. He must be hit. With his right hand he reached over to his left elbow. He slowly ran his hand upward feeling for the wound. When he reached his shoulder, pain exploded as his hand prodded the gouge in his flesh.

As his head cleared, he raised himself to look around. His eyes again fell on the men in the center of the crater. One man was moaning, his body torn apart. Someone was kneeling next to him. He was covered in blood. Others were screaming. Blood, dirt, and debris was everywhere. He couldn't tell who was who. Chaos prevailed.

Thinking more clearly now, Mort knew that in a matter of a few minutes everyone would be dead. *I can just lay here and watch everyone get killed or I can do something.* He took his eyes off the men in the crater and looked toward the top of the hill. Grabbing his rifle, he charged blindly up the hill toward his enemy. The only thing keeping him on his feet was the raw, animal instinct that coursed through his veins.

JR had been watching Mort. He was relieved when he saw him raise his head. His eyes grew big as he watched Mort start toward the hilltop with blood running down his left arm, and his M16 in his right hand.

Hawk could tell the NVA had the hill plotted. The mortars were not random. The NVA were strategically adjusting their aim to pattern the entire hill. A mortar landed close by. He lifted his head to see what was happening beyond his foxhole. He saw Mort stand up and charge the hill. Without a second thought, Hawk was on his feet. As he broke into a run, JR joined him. They caught up with Mort just as he reached the highest point of the hill.

Mort, JR, and Captain Hawk scanned the hillside to find the location of the NVA. A flash of fire and smoke identified where the mortars were coming from. Together they laid out fire in that direction. They poured lead into the area as fast as they could. When Captain Hawk paused to reload his rifle, he realized the mortars had stopped. He put his hand on Mort's bloody shoulder. "It's over."

Mort continued to fire.

"Mort! It's over! You can stop firing."

Mort slowly lowered his rifle. He stared at Captain Hawk.

"It's over, Mort. They stopped firing the mortars."

JR let out a breath as he realized they had stopped the NVA manning the mortar tube. It didn't matter whether they hit them or they retreated. All that mattered was that the mortars stopped. "Let's go back and see what we can do to help the men."

CHAPTER 16

Third Platoon

1516 Hours

Brian crouched next to Mex. "Please, God. Help us! Please!" He broke out in a cold sweat. His stomach felt like lead. "Our Father who art in heaven, hallowed be Thy name. Thy kingdom come. Thy will be done..."

Mex's voice blended with Brian's. "but deliver us from evil. For Thine is the kingdom, and the power, and the glory."

Each time Fabe heard the screeching sound of the mortar, he held his breath. There was no predicting where the mortar was going to land. His knuckles were white from his strong hold on the rifle. Heart pounding painfully. Waiting. Unable to move. Dreading the next scream of men as they were hit. Wondering if it would be him.

Lil' Bro lay in a different turn of the same trench as Fabe. Each time he heard the thoop of the mortar leaving the tube, he involuntarily jumped. *This is it.* He knew he'd never go home alive. Never see his wife. Or his son. Never see another day. He closed his eyes, prepared to die.

Lil' Bro heard screaming. Not just one person, but the sound of many tortured voices. Men yelling for a medic. It seemed like everyone was shouting. Voices were coming from all directions. None of it made sense to him. As he listened to the men calling out, he became aware that the mortars had stopped. He was alive. Slowly raising his head to peek out, he saw Merdis and Clark leap into action as they started running to his right. He didn't want to move. He wanted to stay in the safety of the ditch. But his job was to stay with Merdis. What if Merdis needed the radio?

He looked at the trench behind him. Fabe stood up and

stepped out of the trench. Lil' Bro knew he had to get out, too. He stood on shaking legs. He started running toward Merdis and Clark. His legs felt like rubber. After only a few steps, he stopped. The sight ahead of him was beyond belief. There was blood everywhere. One man with an arm dangling below the gore of ripped up flesh and bone. Another with blood on his head and chest. So many wounded. He didn't know what to do. Turning around, he tried to control the bile rising in his throat. He couldn't bear to look at the gruesome sight one minute longer. He kept his eyes on the ground as he started walking toward the crater. Looking up, he stopped dead in his tracks. Things were even worse in the crater. He saw one man ripped apart, his guts spilling out. Another with a leg blown off. Blood on everyone. More blood than he could imagine. Was this a nightmare? No. It was real. It was war. He couldn't hold the bile back. He puked. How could this happen? He thought the sight of the men on the first day was bad. But this was much worse. It was beyond his wildest imagination. As he stood there looking at the bloody jumble of men, he felt so dizzy he could barely keep on his feet.

Merdis stopped to look for Lil' Bro. He saw him standing up and let out a sigh of relief. The relief turned into fear as he saw him swaying. It looked like he was about to collapse. What was wrong? Was he hit? He ran to him and grabbed his arm to keep him from falling.

Lil' Bro was as white as a ghost. He didn't even realize Merdis was standing beside him.

"Sit down."

Lil' Bro just stared ahead, swaying.

"Sit down. NOW!" Merdis forced Lil' Bro to sit on the ground. "Take some slow, deep breaths."

As Lil' Bro fought to control his breathing, he slowly became aware of his surroundings. His blurred vision began clearing. He looked at Merdis with glassy eyes. "Merdis?"

"Are you ok?" Merdis couldn't see any blood on him.

"Are you hit?"

"No. I'm sorry... So many...."

Merdis let out his breath, relieved that Lil' Bro was okay. He put his arm around him. "It's ok. We're going to be ok now."

"It's just so... I've never seen..."

"I know. Sit here as long as you need to. Breathe slow. Don't try getting up until I come back. I gotta go help the others."

Lil' Bro looked as though he didn't comprehend anything.

"Did you hear me? I said, stay here until I come back."

"Go ahead. I'm ok."

Merdis took off at a run toward the men in the third platoon.

Brian and Mex cautiously got out of their foxhole. Surveying the area near them, they could see that several men from the third platoon were wounded. They looked around for the other three platoons. Men in the crater were screaming. Others were walking around as if in a daze. So many had blood on them. They could see that they hadn't fared any better than the third platoon. Maybe worse.

Since Doc Bauer was sent back, the third platoon had no medic. Brian and Mex knew they had to see if they could help the wounded men. The medics from the other platoons had their hands full. It would be a while before they worked their way over to the third platoon. Brian could see three men lying close together. They were all from the third platoon, but he didn't see anyone from his squad. Thank God for that. He started toward them to see what he could do to help. Each one had blood saturating their fatigues.

One of the men looked up at him. "Help me. Please. Help me," he gasped between breaths. He feebly reached his right arm out to Brian.

Brian recognized him as the guy who took over his

guard duty when he went to the rice paddy to get water. They called him Spinner. Blood was flowing from his head. Part of his skull was missing above his right ear. Swallowing the bile in his throat, Brian knelt beside him. "I'll move you away from here. Somewhere safer."

"NO! Please. Don't make me move. Just don't leave me."

"I won't." Brian knelt down beside the man and supported his bloody head on his lap. God help him! What could he do? He knew the man could not possibly live. All he could do was keep his promise and stay with him.

"I'm cold. Please help me. Don't leave."

"It's ok. I'll stay right here."

"Why is everything so blurry?"

Brian swallowed hard. "I don't know."

"I'm so cold. I'm scared."

Brian looked at the man in his arms. He was so young. He held him tighter.

"Am I dying?"

Brian didn't answer. He couldn't bring himself to say it.

"Please… just tell me. I'm not gonna make it, am I?"

"I don't know."

"Will you write to my mother? Tell her I love her."

"Yes. I'll write to her."

Brian could no longer hold back the tears. "Do you believe in God?"

"Yes."

"The Lord is my shepherd; I shall not want." Brian took a deep breath to calm his shaky voice. "He maketh me to lie down in green pastures: He leadeth me beside the still waters. He restoreth my soul: he leadeth me in the paths of righteousness for his name's sake."

Brian's words became stronger. "Yea, though I walk through the valley of the shadow of death, I will fear no evil: for thou art with me; thy rod and thy staff they comfort me."

Spinner let out three slow gasps as the life left his body. Brian continued to cradle him as tears ran down his face.

"Surely goodness and mercy shall follow me all the days of my life, and I shall dwell in the house of the Lord forever."

Mex could see that all the wounded in the third platoon were being attended to. He saw Fabe standing near the edge of the opening. Fabe had his rifle ready to fire as he scanned the brush in anticipation of an attack from that side.

Mex ran over to Fabe. "I'll help you stand guard from this direction."

Fabe glanced at Mex, then looked around and saw Brian. "Looks like Brian is holding somebody. He looks like he's in pretty rough shape." Even from a distance, Fabe could see the blood on his head.

"Brian is strong. He'll do a good job of comforting him."

Fabe shook his head in agreement. "The way those mortars were coming down, I thought we were all a-goner."

"Me, too. They sure had the hill covered from one side to the other."

"I don't know what the hell stopped 'em."

"I peeked out to see what was happening and saw a couple of guys running up the hill. I don't know who it was. Next thing I knew, the mortars stopped."

"Thank God."

"I can't believe they won't take advantage of this and attack from another direction."

"I hope there's someone watching the jungle side, too."

Merdis and Clark checked on the wounded men from the third platoon. They designated the area at the bottom of the hill by the crumbling wall as a triage area for the wounded men.

Merdis walked over to Fabe and Mex. He called three other men to help them watch the right side of the hill. "Y'all stay here until all the wounded are off the hill."

Merdis and Clark started walking toward the crater.

"I better go check on Lil' Bro." Merdis veered off from the direction he was headed.

"Ok. I'll be in the crater. Looks like they need help."

Merdis found Lil' Bro still sitting where he left him. His color had improved, and he gave Merdis a weak smile. "I'm ok now. I was just going to try to find you to see if you needed me."

"Just stay sitting a while longer."

"What about you?"

"I'm headed to the crater. Looks like they got hit pretty hard."

"I'll come along."

"No. Stay here. There's no need for you to go there. When you're sure you're doin' ok, join the men by the wall."

"What if you need the radio?"

"I'll know where to find you."

Lil' Bro stared at the rice paddy to his south. He turned his head to look at the men from the third platoon, then the men in the crater. Because he was sitting on the ground, he didn't have a full view of the wounded men. He didn't need to see more. He had already seen more than enough. Enough killing. Enough pain. Enough living in fear.

He wanted to escape from this living hell. He wanted to go home to his wife and son. How he had changed in the month he'd been in Vietnam. There were so many things he'd never take for granted again. Drinking cool water — all the water you wanted. Taking a bath. Eating a hot meal. Sleeping in a bed. Sleeping with his wife.

At least he had survived. So far. When he saw Cindy again, he'd kiss her like he'd never done before. How he longed to hold her in his arms. She'd been his sweetheart since they started high school. They were both in the marching band. She played the clarinet and he played the trumpet. Every time the band went somewhere to march in a parade or go to a competition, they sat together on the bus. They'd hold hands and talk. At first it was silly talk. By the time they were seniors in high school, they talked about a future together. He wanted to be an engineer. She wanted to have lots of kids. It all seemed so simple then. Now she was on the other side of the world, living with her parents. He was stuck in the middle of a war. Nothing was simple now.

CHAPTER 17

Mortar Platoon

MEANWHILE...

Most of the mortar platoon was inside the bomb crater. Cooper, like the others in the crater, tried to make himself a small target by lying prone on the ground. The second mortar landed only a meter to his left. The energy expended by the explosion threw him into the air. He landed on his butt with a forceful thud. Pain exploded in his lower spine and radiated up his back. His breath came in jagged bursts. He didn't feel pain from the wound in his chest or notice the blood on his shirt. Waiting for the severe back pain to subside, he sat motionless as his left arm hung limply by his side. The last thing he remembered before he blacked out was the explosion of another mortar.

Deadeye's rucksack was where he had dropped it prior to joining Amos. Looking back at his rucksack, he wondered if he could get to it and grab some shells for the recoilless. If he could find Chief, maybe they could fire back over the hill. As he was ready to make a dive for the rucksack, another mortar exploded. The rucksack jumped into the air as it was blown to kingdom come. His heart skipped a beat, as he realized how close he had come to being blown away. Looking to his right, he saw a small depression in the crater. Or was it just his imagination? No matter, he was going there. He had nothing to lose. Staying low to the ground, he scrambled for the depression. When he reached it, he took a fetal position and waited for the inevitable. As the ground shook a third time, everything became blurry before he passed out.

Chief was on the ground only a few feet from Cooper.

The ground shook. He knew the explosion had to be close to him. Raising his head, he looked around to see if anyone around him was hit. Cooper, to his right, had a significant amount of blood on his chest. Lifting his head higher, he tried to see how seriously he was hit. Before he could fully focus on Cooper, Chief was thrown two feet into the air as the next mortar landed. It felt like someone hit him with a baseball bat in the back of his neck. *They've blown my head off! No. My head must still be attached. I can think.*

Slowly Chief reached up to feel the back of his head. *Well, my head is still there.* He felt the warmth of the blood on his fingers. He probed the area. As his finger found a hole in the back of his neck, his world went black.

Brooklyn winced as mortar rounds landed. He knew the NVA were adjusting their aim after each mortar hit. He'd done the same with High Angle Hell in the past. They fired off several rounds, then a pause came while they made adjustments. This is what he'd been waiting for. Jumping up, he shouted, "Get off the hill, they have it patterned!"

Everyone stayed cowered down. Brooklyn turned in all directions. Why wasn't anyone moving? "Get off the hill!"

He ran toward the center of the crater. "Get off the hill! They have it patterned!"

Nearly stumbling over a body, he stopped, temporarily paralyzed. He couldn't believe what he was seeing. Dan's body was split apart. He was gasping for air. Obviously, he had taken a near direct hit from a mortar. Brooklyn stepped around the body and took three more steps before collapsing. He was only vaguely aware that mortars continued to pound the hillside. The sight of Dan's mangled body overtook his mind. He was motionless. *How could this happen?* He felt like the world was crumbling around him. He wasn't shaking. He wasn't afraid. He wasn't crying. Nothing. He just laid there in stunned silence.

The mortars stopped. Rico ignored the pain in his back and buttocks as he hobbled toward the wounded men, leaving his piece of High Angle Hell behind. He knew some shrapnel hit him, but that had to wait until later. The first man he came across was from the other squad in the mortar platoon. He recognized him as a friend of Mort and Amos. The man was hit in his back leg near his buttocks. "I'll get a medic. You're gonna be ok."

As Rico started out to find a medic, he realized they were all knee deep in blood. They never looked up as they tended the wounded. Rico returned alone. The best he could do was to keep his eyes on the medic and get him as soon as he had a chance.

"Where's the medic?"

"It might be a few minutes before he gets here. I'll stay with you." Rico got out his first aid pouch and held a dressing over the wound on the man's upper leg.

Hawk turned from the hill and ran to the foxhole he had been in with Major Close. Close had a significant amount of blood on his right upper arm. "You're hurt."

"It's not that bad. Just some shrapnel in my arm. I'm okay."

"It doesn't look okay to me." Hawk grabbed his C scarf to wrap his arm just above the elbow.

"Don't worry about me. I told you, I'm okay." He pointed to the nearest foxhole with his left hand. "I haven't seen any movement from that hole. I know there was someone in it. You better check that out first."

The color drained from Hawk's face as he realized that Close was referring to the hole that he almost jumped into with his FO. As he stood up, he could see that the far side of the foxhole had partially caved in. His heart pounded as he walked over with leaden feet. He swallowed hard as he saw the bodies of two men. Neither was moving. Were they dead? No. They couldn't both be dead… Or could they?

There was a chance one of the men was alive. Hawk jumped into the foxhole. His FO was slumped over, laying across his RTO. Grabbing his shoulders, he sat him up so he could see his face. Grey eyes were staring into oblivion. His face as white as snow.

Hawk looked at his RTO. His head was bloody and cocked in an unnatural position. No chance he was alive, either.

Hawk took a deep breath. Right now he did not have the luxury to grieve. He was responsible for all of Charlie Company. There were men in the crater, and he knew they had been hit hard. He needed to help them. They needed him to be strong.

He willed his legs to stand, but he couldn't move. He squatted down and covered his face with his hands. He couldn't stop the tears. *God, help me. Please, help me to be strong for my men. They've been so brave. Help me. Please, tell me what to do for them.*

After a few minutes Hawk collected himself and started toward the bomb crater.

By the time Hawk reached the crater, his men had sprung into action. Some were yelling for medics while comforting the wounded men, or trying to stop the bleeding as best they could. He could see that the losses were significant. This was the most casualties he'd ever seen in one day.

As Mort ran to the crater, he could hear the men screaming. The first man he came to was someone he recognized from the first platoon. Part of his torso and his buttock was severely severed. He could see that he was dead. Panic engulfed him as he searched for Amos.

He found Amos lying only a few meters away. He was alone. Why wasn't someone helping him? Running to him, Mort gasped as he saw his injuries.

Amos was covered with sand that was mixed with blood. His insides were outside. His left leg was gone, and bones were exposed. The stump of his leg was flailing back and forth.

Mort kneeled next to Amos. "It's ok, buddy. The medic will be here soon."

"Mort?" Amos whispered.

Mort could barely hear him. He squatted beside him and held him. "I'm here." *I can't believe this. He has only a few weeks left. We've been talking about his wedding in October. Most of us got Dear John letters, but Judy remained faithful. She's waiting for him. Will she want him if he only has one leg?*

Amos broke Mort's reverie. "Mort. Tell Judy I love her."

Mort looked at Amos and suddenly realized that the leg was the least of his problems. "I will, Amos. I will."

Studying Amos, Mort knew there was nothing anyone could do to patch him up. Nothing he could do. Nothing the medic could do. Nothing could save his dying friend.

Mort didn't feel the blood running down his arm, or hear the men screaming around him. The only thing he was aware of was Amos. He listened to his labored breaths. He held him close. He didn't try to stop the tears running down his face as he held his dying friend.

Mort was aware that someone was touching his shoulder. He had no idea how long he had been sitting there with Amos.

"Are you ok?" JR was kneeling beside him.

"It's Amos.... I got to help him. He's..."

"There's nothing more you can do, Mort. He's gone."

Mort bowed his head and held his friend close. "Why? Why Amos?"

"I don't know. I'm so sorry."

Tears streamed down Mort's face. He held his friend tightly. "Why? Why not me?"

JR felt the same way. Why not him? "I don't know, Mort. God has a reason he's kept you alive. He has a plan for you."

Mort nodded in agreement, but his mind was not in agreement. *It's not fair. Why, God? Why?*

"Mort, you're hit. You need to get a medic to look at your shoulder."

Mort was unable to move. *Why Amos, of all people? First Sanchez. Now Amos? Why wasn's I killed along with my friends? What right do I have to live?*

"Come on, Mort. Let's do something about that shoulder."

"Just leave me alone." He continued to hold Amos, sobs wracking his body.

JR walked away in silence.

When Chief came to, he saw blood on his shirt and hand. It seemed like there was blood on everything. Again, he reached up and touched the hole in the back of his neck. While it hurt like hell, he realized that he was going to make it.

Only a meter from him he saw Cooper. It looked like he was still in a daze. He was lying on his back gasping for breath and there was a significant amount of blood on his shirt. Chief crawled over to Cooper and turned him onto his right side. His breathing improved. "I'll find a medic."

"Help me. I can't move my arm."

"I'm gonna find a medic. I'll be right back."

"Please... hurry."

Chief was afraid that if he stood up, he'd pass out again. He spotted a medic off to his right. As he started crawling in that direction, he saw Dan lying on the ground about four meters away. He could see his left butt was blown off. The hip joint and tendons were exposed. As he drew closer, he could see that Dan had open wounds everywhere on his torso. His left leg was trying to push and his right arm was flailing around as if he was trying to crawl somewhere. *Where is the damn medic? Dan needs him worse than Cooper.*

Chief had forgotten about his head wound. He tried to stand and run. After only two steps the world started to spin. His vision was blurring. As he fell to his knees, he spotted someone. It looked like Deadeye. He, too, was lying still. He could see blood on his pants and shirt.

Chief took some slow breaths. His vision started to clear. His eyes focused on Deadeye. As he stared at him, he could see that he was breathing. *Thank God he's alive!*

He tried to stand again, but as dizziness overtook him, he collapsed to the ground.

JR saw Chief fall. He rushed over to him to make sure he was breathing. He still had his rucksack on, so JR turned him and managed to remove it. As he rolled him over he saw the bloody area at the back of his neck. He took out his field dressing and applied pressure to the area. He'd stay with him until a medic could come to check him out.

Mort gently laid Amos on the ground. In a daze, he started stumbling around, going in no particular direction. He almost tripped over Dan. Stopping just in time, he saw Dan gasping for air. He could see his body had been almost torn apart.

He knelt down beside Dan. He raised his head, hoping it might help him breathe. But even as he did so, he realized that Dan was dying. "No. Not you, too."

Mort held him as he took his last breath. He sat there for a few minutes, rocking back and forth. He gently lowered his head onto the ground. "How can this be?"

He stood up and started walking. It didn't matter where. He just needed to get away from this. He didn't want to watch any more men die.

Deadeye saw Mort heading in his direction.

"Mort! Over here."

Mort stumbled over to Deadeye. He could see blood on his left arm and leg. At least he didn't look like he was dying.

"Mort. I need to talk to you."

Mort kneeled beside Deadeye. "Are you ok?"

"I'll be ok. Can you find Brooklyn for me?"

Mort was still stunned. He had no idea who he had seen. Except for Amos and Dan. "I haven't seen him."

"What about Dan? I need to talk to him."

"What?"

"Have you seen Dan?"

"Ya. I saw him." He couldn't say the words. He couldn't make himself say Dan was dead.

"Tell him to come here."

Mort looked at Deadeye. "He's busy… he can't come right now."

"I don't think I can walk. I need to talk to Dan before they send me out. Please. Just get him."

"He can't come over here right now... He just can't come." Mort stood and walked away. Deadeye stared at him wondering what was wrong with Mort. It never occurred to him that his best friend might be dead.

Hawk went from man to man trying to assess the casualties. He was almost through the area inside the crater when he came across his RTO. He had a bandage wrapped around his abdomen. Hawk squatted down to talk to him.

"We'll get you out of here as soon as we can."

"I don't think I'm gonna make it."

"You'll make it. I'm going to call for a dustoff now. Hang in there."

Hawk stood up. He grabbed the nearest man that was not injured. "I need you to carry the radio for me. Grab the one from my RTO and follow me." He pointed to the man lying only a few feet away.

Hawk started barking out orders. "Let's get the wounded off the hill. Put them on the other side of the wall. If you're hurt and you can walk, start down. Leave your gear. Someone will pick it up for you. Keep some men watching our perimeter. After all the men are off the hill, start picking up the other stuff — weapons, rucksacks, and anything else you see. Don't leave anything behind. Hurry it up. We're easy pickings if we stay here."

CHAPTER 18

Aftermath

1545 Hours

Merdis and Clark ran toward the men in the crater. They came across Deadeye first. They could see that his wounds were not life-threatening, so they decided to get him off the hill. The medics could tend to him there.

Merdis squatted beside Deadeye. "We'll get you outta here."

"No! I need to talk to Dan. I think Mort went to get him."

"He'll have to find you by the wounded." Clark looked at Merdis. "Let's stand him up.

As they got him to his feet, his knees buckled under him. "Son-of-a-bitch! Just leave me."

"We need to clear the hill. It's too dangerous here. We'll carry you. Just hold on."

Deadeye moaned in pain as they grabbed him by his armpits and feet. "That hurts like hell."

They didn't have the luxury of giving Deadeye any sympathy. They needed to get the hill cleared. They started toward the crumbling wall, ignoring Deadeye's swearing.

While Fabe, Lil' Bro, and others stood watch at the sides of the hill, the rest of the men wasted no time in carrying the wounded to the wall. The wall would give them some shelter, and it would be much easier to guard the perimeter once they were back in this morning's position.

After the wounded were off the hill, the men started gathering the equipment and debris that was left behind. Rucksacks, rifles, and pieces of High Angle Hell were piled together to the right of the wall next to the bodies of those killed in action.

Hawk sent a few men back to search the hill for any smaller items left behind. Nothing could be left for the NVA. They would pick up anything and use it. Anything with metal would be used in homemade landmines and booby traps. They would also scrounge for any ammo or food.

Now that the wounded were gathered behind the wall, the medics began going from man to man in an organized fashion. They checked every wound to be sure it had a proper dressing, and gave morphine to ease the pain. The medics knew their supplies were getting low. If they had not been resupplied that morning, they would not have had enough bandages or morphine to go around. Hopefully, they would be able to evacuate the wounded soon.

At 1600 hours Hawk requested a dustoff with gunships as escorts. He had called in earlier to report that they had a mortar attack with casualties, but at that time he had no idea how many. He turned towards Major Close, who was waiting for the results of the request. "TOC was shocked by the number of casualties we have. I told them I estimated twenty. I asked for three choppers to evacuate everyone, plus gunships. They said they didn't have that many birds available, but they'll do what they can. They'll update me ASAP."

"If we don't get some of these guys out soon, our death toll will go up."

"I was clear about the urgency of the dustoff. I believe they understood." Hawk noticed Close was holding his bandaged arm close to his body. "How's that arm doing?"

"It hurts like hell." Close was guarding his right arm where he was hit with large pieces of shrapnel. It was wrapped with a makeshift bandage from a first aid kit. It looked like he had wrapped it himself.

"I'll get the medic to give you some morphine and put on a proper dressing."

"Don't worry about that. I'm fine. Just let the medics tend to the others."

"I'm going to get a medic."

"You will NOT get a medic for me. That's an order, Captain."

Hawk glared at Major Close.

"An order. Understand?"

"Yes, Sir."

Time seemed to stand still as Hawk waited for a response. After only five minutes had passed, he had his answer. He had a smile on his face as he turned to Close. "The Blue Ghosts will accompany the dustoff. They only have one chopper available to pick up the casualties. After they load the first group of men, they will take them to the medical aid station at LZ Baldy. After they unload, they will return with the Blue Ghosts to pick up the second load. We need to make sure we get all the men on the choppers that we can. They will only make two trips in."

Captain Hawk met with the platoon and squad leaders. He informed them of the choppers that would be coming in for the dustoff.

"Merdis, I want you and Turner to figure out how many we need to send out, and how we can get the most men on the choppers. I don't care how you do it, but I don't want to be stuck carrying around men like we did a few days ago."

"Yes, Sir. We're on it."

"Good. After that, I want you to assign men to carry the wounded and dead to the chopper. Let the men know what order they're to load them."

"Yes, Sir."

"We will not send their rucksacks or rifles. We need every inch of space for the men."

"The second platoon will provide security. Keep an eye out for Bravo Company. I expect them to be coming through the jungle anytime."

JR was standing by the wounded men. He squatted by Mort, who was sitting down with his back against the crumbling wall. Blood was seeping through the bandage on his shoulder.

"Need a cigarette?"

Mort nodded.

JR sat down next to Mort. Pulling out a cigarette, he held it to his lips to light it. He handed the lit cigarette to Mort.

"Thanks."

"You saved our bacon today."

"Hell, I didn't even know what I was doing. I was closest to the hilltop. It was instinct. I figured run and get the bastards or get hit with a mortar. Anyhow, you and Hawk were there, too. I didn't do it alone."

"No. But you're the one that started charging up the hill. I never would have had the guts to do it if you hadn't taken the lead."

Mort took a long drag from his cigarette. "Did you see Amos?"

JR saw the pain in Mort's eyes. He nodded.

"And Dan? They were both blown all to hell."

JR lit a cigarette for himself to calm his nerves.

"Amos asked me to tell Judy he loves her." They both sat quietly as tears ran down Mort's cheeks.

Mort looked accusingly at JR. "Nobody in the mortar platoon gets killed, huh?"

JR closed his eyes. He felt terrible. It wasn't like he intentionally lied to Mort. No one in the mortar platoon had been killed the entire time he'd been in Nam. He'd just been trying to comfort Mort after he lost Sanchez. But he was wrong. Dead wrong. "I'm sorry... I'm sorry I said that. I lied to you. I really didn't mean to."

"Forget it. It wasn't your fault. It's just the fuckin' war."

After JR finished his cigarette, he got up and walked over to Cooper and Chief. He knelt down between them.

"Cigarette?"

Cooper looked up at him, running his bloody fingers through his hair. His left arm hung limply at his side. "Yes."

JR handed him a cigarette and lit it.

"Are they gonna get us out?"

"Yup. My job is to see that Chief gets on the chopper."

Chief knew he was weak. He'd lost a lot of blood. But he was determined to get to the chopper on his own. "I can walk, ya know."

"They have it all planned out. Everyone is assigned to helping people on the chopper. Since you keep blacking out, I have to make sure you get on the chopper. And in the right order. It just makes my job all the easier if you can get there by yourself."

Deadeye was laying where Clark and Merdis had put him next to the wounded men in the third platoon. A cigarette was dangling from his mouth as he saw Fabe walking by.

"Fabe!"

Fabe turned and walked over to Deadeye. He had bandages on his left arm and leg. There was blood all over his pants and shirt. He looked relaxed, almost sleepy. Must be the morphine. "Whatcha need?"

"Where's Dan? I need to talk to him."

"I ain't seen him. But, hell, that don't mean nothin'. I been keepin' watch on the perimeter."

"Can you find him for me? I gotta tell him I'm goin' home."

"I can't look for him right now. I gotta go. Merdis is waiting for me with orders. If I see Dan, I'll send him your way."

Merdis and Clark worked together to organize the dustoff. There would be eleven on the first chopper, and twelve on the second one. They would load the dead first. Then the wounded. Those who were able to walk would go on next, except one person who would sit by the door. Last would be the ones with most severe injuries. They were last because they needed to be unloaded first. If all went as planned everyone would get out, except those with very minor injuries.

The area for the chopper was being secured by the second platoon. The men had the wounded and dead lined up so they would go on in the specified order. Clark hoped they could cram the men in like he planned.

"Choppers coming!"

At 1635 the Blue Ghosts arrived. While the other chopper hovered over the landing area, the Blue Ghosts circled the area just outside the landing area. They continuously fired into the surrounding area to deter any interference by the NVA.

The men of Charlie Company swiftly loaded the chopper waiting to pick up the wounded and dead. They managed to get all eleven men on the chopper, including Rico and Chief. The choppers took off toward LZ Baldy.

Chief was going in and out of consciousness. He was awake when the chopper landed. Sitting up, he moved to the edge of the chopper with the intent of walking into the hospital. As he stood up, the world left him and he crumbled to the ground. The medical staff picked him up and loaded him on a gurney. The next time he opened his eyes, he was lying naked on a surgical table. The last thing he heard before he lost consciousness was the nurse. "We'll take care of you. You're gonna be ok."

In the field, Merdis was barking out orders. "Get the rest of the wounded lined up for the next chopper! Move your asses! I don't want any fuck-ups."

Twenty minutes later the Blue Ghosts returned with the chopper, constantly firing into the surrounding area to discourage any interference by the NVA. As the empty chopper hovered, Dan's body was loaded on the right side of the chopper and placed on top of another corpse. Mort was first on from the left side of the chopper, as his wounds were less significant. Deadeye was placed in the center of the chopper next to the bodies. Again, the most severely wounded were loaded last, with the exception of Major Close. He waited until last to be sure everyone else got on. The chopper began its assent. The door gunner noticed that the body on the top was rocking back and forth. He tapped Deadeye on the shoulder. "Grab this guy's belt so he doesn't fall out."

Deadeye took his right hand and grabbed the belt. As his eyes wandered to the man's face, he went white. *Oh my God! It can't be. Not Dan.* Tears ran down his face. He felt lightheaded. He took deep breaths to keep from passing out. This was his worst nightmare.

Mort watched as medical staff ran to the choppers with wheelchairs and gurneys. The most severely wounded were taken directly to the surgical areas. Deadeye was taken in by wheelchair, and quickly disappeared around the corner.

Mort was the last one of the wounded to get off the chopper. He started walking toward the medical facility. It seemed like it was miles, although it was only twenty meters away. He was directed to a waiting room where he joined Major Close. He knew it would be a while before he was treated because his injuries were not as severe as others. Fortunately, he did not know what was ahead of him. After they removed the shrapnel and dressed his shoulder, he would be sent to a bunker for the night. Later, he would be asked to go to the morgue and identify the bodies.

As the last chopper pulled out the point man from Bravo Company stepped out of the jungle. Normally their appearance would have brought a cheer from Charlie Company. Right now no one felt like cheering.

Hawk walked over to talk to the Lieutenant in charge of Bravo Company. Their company commander had been wounded and sent to the rear. Hawk brought him up to date on the day's events. Bravo was down to about sixty men. They would be spending the night with Charlie Company.

They would only have to dig a few foxholes; the rest could use the ones vacated by the men sent out on the dustoff.

Hawk assembled his platoon leaders, "I want a count of how many we have left in each platoon. Move all of Charlie Company to the foxholes to the east. Three men in each hole. Bravo will take the remaining holes and dig more, as needed. They will be staying with our company until we receive further orders. We're really fortunate to be joining forces."

Within fifteen minutes the platoon leaders had reported to Hawk. There were forty-seven men left in Charlie Company. Combined with Bravo they had the equivalent of one functioning unit. Hawk sat down and looked at his men. They were holding up remarkably well. He was proud of every one of them. Today had been hard on everyone. He'd taken more casualties than he had in the last six months. All in just a few minutes. But they'd done what they had to do. Every day of this mission had been a challenge. And it wasn't over yet. Looking down at his hands, he saw dried blood. He took his canteen and washed some of the blood away. He wiped his hands on his C scarf. As he studied his hands, his eyes went to his wedding ring. What was Mary doing right now? It was nighttime at home. Or early morning. Mary always looked so beautiful in the morning. When he was home, she always got up with him no matter how early he had to report for duty. They'd have a cup of coffee together before he started his day. Then she'd send him off with a kiss. He sure longed for her kisses now. Soon he'd be seeing her in Hawaii. He had to think positive. Now that they were joined with Bravo the chances of getting out alive were improving.

Merdis was the first of the platoon leaders to join Hawk. "The men are all in their assigned fox holes, Sir."

"Good job, Merdis. What about the personal things and weapons from the men we sent out?"

"They're piled by the wall."

"Go through the rucksacks and take out any personal items. Put them together into one or two rucksacks."

"Yes, sir."

By now all the platoon leaders had joined them. "Instruct your men that they'll need to carry all they can when we move out." Hawk smiled. "You guys did great today. After you've assigned men to go through the rucksacks that were left behind, get settled in your foxhole. Eat something and rest up for whatever comes next."

"Yes, Sir."

Fabe lit a chunk of C4 to warm some water. He'd have coffee and a cigarette before it got dark. He wasn't hungry. Yesterday he'd have given almost anything for food. Now that they were resupplied, he didn't have an appetite. He was sitting on the edge of his foxhole. Brian was reading his Bible. Mex was taking watch.

He looked over at Lil' Bro in the next foxhole. He was holding up better than expected. "Hey Bro! You made it!"

Lil' Bro looked up at Fabe. "So far. The day's not over yet."

"It'll be a long night for sure. At least we have food and water."

Lil' Bro took out his pen and paper and started writing.

Fabe knew he was writing to his wife. He took out the letter Lil' Bro had given him that morning. "Here. You can take this back now."

"You keep it. We're not outta here yet."

Fabe kept the letter. Lil' Bro had reason to be concerned. They were trapped in this hellhole with nowhere to go. As he tucked the letter to the side of the rucksack, his hand brushed against a book. He pulled out his Bible and opened it. It fell open to Isaiah chapter forty-one. *"Fear thou not; for I am with thee: be not dismayed; for I am thy God: I will strengthen thee; yea, I will help thee; yea, I will uphold thee with the right hand of my righteousness"*. He looked up. Brian was watching him. He smiled, knowing Brian was right.

JR and Brooklyn were in the same foxhole. They were both exhausted. It had been a hard day for the mortar platoon. They had only seven of the eighteen men they started out with. Their platoon and squad leaders were all gone. JR had been assigned to be the acting platoon leader. The recoilless had been damaged, rendering it useless. High Angle Hell had a dent in the tube, so it was also out of commission.

JR looked at Brooklyn who sat crouched in the foxhole. He was sobbing. As far as JR was concerned, he'd take watch all night if he had to. He wouldn't sleep anyway. Maybe when Brooklyn was cried out, he'd fall asleep. In any case, it would be a long, difficult night.

CHAPTER 19

What Are Our Chances?

9 March 1969 – 0615 Hours

Fabe awoke with the sun shining in his eyes. He had to blink a few times before he could focus. The sun hadn't reached Mex on the other side of the foxhole, he was still dozing.

"Mornin'. I'm glad you finally got a little shuteye." Brian smiled as Fabe stood up in the foxhole. "Better have a cup of coffee and eat something before you take over watch."

"I can't believe we made it through the night without an attack."

"Me either. I'm glad Bravo was here. Maybe that helped discourage 'em. If it was just the few of us from Charlie, I bet they would have attacked."

Fabe looked at his wrist watch. "It's O six fifteen! Why the hell didn't you wake me? It's past time for me to take over."

"As long as you were sleeping, I thought I'd let you be. It looked like you didn't sleep at all until about five o'clock. We've hardly slept all week. Anyway, what's fifteen minutes? Take your time and eat. Once everyone is up and about we won't really have to worry about it. Now that Bravo has joined us, there's plenty of eyes to watch."

"Aren't you hungry?"

"Na. I had some pound cake a little while ago."

"Okay, then. I'm making coffee. Maybe I'll actually warm up some food, too. It might taste good."

"I wouldn't go so far as to say that."

Brooklyn reached for his rucksack. It was well past midnight when exhaustion finally overtook him and he fell asleep. At 0400 hours he took over watch. Now he sat outside the foxhole, eating for the first time since the mortar attack. Suddenly he was famished.

JR woke up as the sun reached his eyes. "What time is it?"

"Must be 'bout six toirty."

JR looked up at the sky. There wasn't a cloud to be seen. The mist was lifting off the hillside. "It's gonna be a hot one today."

"At least we got watta."

"I'm makin' some cocoa. Want some?"

"Sure do."

Brooklyn got out his cup. "God, I just can't get 'em outta my mind. That mawhta attack was awful. I've nevuh seen anythin' like it."

"I know. It's hard to believe."

"I don't see how the mawhtas missed me."

"Me either. Did you see my pot?" JR handed his helmet to Brooklyn.

"Holy shit!" Brooklyn took the helmet from JR and studied it. The camouflage fabric that had covered the pot was shredded and hanging in jagged strips. Most of the paint was off and it was filled with dents all over the top.

"The debris hit my head so hard that I thought I was hit. All I took was a little shrapnel in my neck. And look at my fingernails." He held out his hands so Brooklyn could see the dirt embedded under his fingernails.

"If yuh took shrapnel, yuh shoulda got outta here on the dustoff."

"It ain't that bad. The choppers were full. Anyway, somebody had to stay here and keep you in line."

JR handed Brooklyn a cup of cocoa. He took a sip from his cup. "Did you see 'What Did You Do in the War, Daddy?'"

"Never hoid of it."

"It was a movie. Came out a coupla years ago."

"No, I din't see it."

"It was a comedy about World War II. Like war was fun. After watching that, I thought it might not be so bad to be in the Army. Let me tell you, life in Nam is nothing like that movie."

"I mostly went tuh the drive-in."

"I bet you weren't alone when you went there."

"The goil I liked tuh take was more interestin' than any movie. You could say she entertained me."

"Oh-la-la. Who doesn't like taking a doll to the drive-in?"

"She was a hellava goil. She didn't hold nuttin' back, neitha."

"I took a girl, Rosemary I think her name was, to see "The Graduate". I have no idea what the movie was about. But I sure remember Rosemary."

"I love the drive-in movies. Best place in the world tuh make out with your goil."

Clark smiled as Hawk approached him. "Mornin', Captain."

"Clark."

It was unusual for Hawk to call him by his first name. Obviously, he wasn't here to give orders. "What's up?"

"Nothin' new. The men are restless. I'm sure you've noticed."

"If you don't mind my saying so, they have plenty of reasons to be restless." Clark took a drag from his cigarette.

Hawk looked Clark in the eye. "I don't know how long we can stay here. When I talked to TOC, I got the impression that the big boys in the back couldn't agree on how to proceed."

"The way I see it, they either have to send in reinforcements or pull us out."

"I agree."

"Damn it, Captain! Haven't we had enough? What are they waiting for?"

"We've had more than enough as far as I'm concerned. But I'm not the one making the calls."

"It's almost noon. I hope they decide soon. Sitting here is wearing on everyone's nerves."

"I know. I realize there's only ten men left in the third platoon, but try to keep their spirits up."

"Yes, sir, I sure as hell will."

As Hawk walked away, Clark got up and walked over to Merdis. Lil' Bro, Brian, and Fabe were standing close by.

"Hey, Merdis!'

"Ya?"

"Did I ever tell you about the time I went into a bar and there were three marines sitting there?"

Merdis smiled. He could use a joke right now. "No. Tell me about it."

"Well I went into this bar called the Korn Krib. Everyone went there. So, I saw some guys sittin' at a table. I sat down at the bar, ordered a beer, and looked 'em over. Then I started talkin' to one of 'em. I said to one guy, "Wanna hear a joke about Marine guys?" The guy said, "Well, before you tell that joke, you should know somethin'. I'm 6'1, 200 lbs., and I'm a Marine. The guy sitting next to me is 6'3, weighs 220, and he's a Marine. The fellow next to him is 6'10, weighs 270, and he's also a Marine. Now, you still wanna tell that joke?"

I said 'Nah, I don't want to have to explain it three times.'"

The guys all chuckled.

As Clark walked away with Merdis, Lil' Bro turned to Fabe. "What'll happen now? Will they send us up the hill again?"

"Not likely. But you never know."

"I better go finish my letter to Cindy so it's ready to mail when we get back."

"Well, well. Now you think you might make it?"

Lil' Bro shook his head. "I don't know. Yesterday, I sure thought it was my last. Since I survived that — who knows? Maybe I will make it."

Fabe watched Lil' Bro walk away. He was a helluva nice kid. He hoped he'd make it.

Brian was still standing next to Fabe. "We might's well sit down. Who knows how much walking we'll have to do yet today."

Fabe took out a cigarette as they sat down a couple of meters from their foxhole. After lighting it, he took out his calendar from his wallet and marked off another day. "We're over a fourth of the way."

"Huh?"

"We've been in Nam for over three months."

"Yup. Three months and seven days to be exact."

"We'll be home before Thanksgiving."

"And deer hunting. I always come to Wisconsin to hunt with my uncle."

"I didn't know you had an uncle in Wisconsin."

"Really? I thought I told you. He lives near a little town called Winneconne."

"Hell, that's less than an hour from me."

"We can get together when I'm there."

"My folks have plenty'a room. You can stay with us anytime."

"You live on a farm, don't ya?"

"We live in the country. It used to be a farm. When I was little, I had bad allergies. I had eczema really bad. Hell, I was in the hospital for six weeks. They said it was because of the damn cows on the farm. So, my old man sold the cattle and went to work in the foundry. Now we only raise chickens, ducks, and pigs."

"You got a lot of land?"

"Prolly a hundred acres. The old man plants stuff to sell. Ma cans a lot of stuff. The rest is woodland. Good hunting."

"Does she make dill pickles?"

"Yup. Dill pickles, sweet pickles, beets, sauerkraut. Lots of stuff."

"I bet she's a good cook."

"Really good."

"Then I'm definitely coming to visit."

"I'm gonna hold you to that."

Hawk watched helicopters flying low. After talking to TOC, he learned that the Warlords scout helicopters had been called in for a "sniffer mission". The goal was to determine the presence and location of enemy units. The helicopter crews would report to TOC. They would use that information to determine if it was feasible to extract the 1/52. It would also tell them where they might be able to land a chopper successfully.

The orders everyone had been waiting for came at 1500 hours. Captain Hawk met with his platoon and squad leaders. "TOC has decided to evacuate all of the 1/52nd. They will be moving Delta Company off Professional and sending them to LZ Baldy. Alpha Company will be picked up later this afternoon. Bravo Company will be moving out soon. They have to be at an assigned area tonight so they can be lifted out first thing in the morning. We're to stay here tonight, and in the morning proceed to our area of evacuation. When we get there, hopefully before noon, they'll pick us up. Any questions?"

JR wanted more details. "Why's Delta going to Baldy?"

"Professional has been hit really hard. Delta is down to half their size. They're sending the entire 198th to Baldy."

"Who'll be on Professional?"

"The 196th."

"Why can't we stay with Bravo? It seems to me that would be safer."

"TOC feels it's safest moving in small groups. When the choppers come in to pick us up, they don't want to make so many trips, either. That would just set us up as a target."

Merdis frowned. "If we have to stay here overnight, and we're not getting picked up until noon tomorrow, can't they send in some kind of reinforcements? We're so small. We're likely to be overrun."

"They have no one to send in. Everyone is either in the field or dwindled down. We're on our own. If necessary, we'll fight our way out as best we can."

"We'll move out at first light tomorrow." Hawk pulled out a map and gave the men the coordinates. He pointed to an area on the map. It will take us at least three hours to get there."

Clark studied the map. "It shouldn't take three hours. That is, providing we survive tonight."

Hawk ignored Clark's comment. "Have your men gather all the rifles, the rucksacks with personal items, and any other items left behind by those who were evacuated. We'll carry all we can with us tomorrow. That'll slow us down. We'll need to take frequent breaks. Whatever can't be carried will need to be destroyed and buried. Get on it."

The remaining men of Charlie Company somberly watched Bravo pack up. Soon they disappeared into the jungle where they had come from nearly twenty-four hours ago.

Fabe offered to stay near their foxhole and keep an eye on the perimeter. Now that they were a small force, they'd have to be extra diligent in watching for any signs of the enemy. Mex and Brian headed over to where they had stashed the extra rucksacks and rifles.

Merdis and Clark took charge. Merdis looked at Brian and Mex. "Y'all take a rucksack and two rifles. Take one of 'em to Fabe. Grab extra ammo and another rifle if you can manage it."

Mex and Brian carried their load back to their foxhole. "We brought you a present."

Fabe just kept staring outside their perimeter watching

for the enemy. He was certain they would be showing up soon. "What about extra ammo?"

"If you want ammo or another rifle, we'll get it. We didn't know how much you wanted to carry."

"I sure as hell don't want the fuckin' NVA getting their hands on it."

Mex chimed in. "They're gonna burn what we don't take along. Since we were resupplied yesterday, we can't carry a lot extra. I thought I might go back for a couple extra bandoleers. You want me to bring ammo for you? Or a rifle?"

"Bring an extra bandoleer. I might need it. Two rifles are enough to carry. And a canteen of water, if there's extra."

When Brian and Mex returned, they sat on the edge of the foxhole. They sat down the extra bandoleers and four canteens of water. Mex took one of the canteens and warmed some water for coffee. Next, they warmed some rations.

Brian was studying the surrounding landscape. "I doubt anyone will sleep tonight. I know I won't. I got the heebie-jeebies again. I just don't feel good about this."

"Me either." Fabe whipped out a cigarette and his Zippo lighter.

Mex finished his coffee and got out a pencil and paper.

"You gonna write your old lady?"

"Yup. Sure do miss her."

"I miss lots of things." Fabe sent a ring of smoke in the air.

"What do you miss most?"

"I dunno. Sleeping in a bed. My mother's cooking. Cold water. Hot showers. Girls. Cars. Take your pick."

Mex turned to Brian. "What about you?"

"Going to church, and sleeping. I don't think I've had a good night's sleep since I got here. What about you, Mex?"

"Sleeping. With my wife. Boy, I sure miss her."

Fabe decided to check on Lil' Bro. "What's up, Bro?"

"I been thinking about the last few days. It all seems so unreal. Like I'm not even really here. You ever feel that way?"

"Sure. Can't help it."

"A few days ago, I thought it was bad. Carrying the guys around for days. Mud and blood crusted on my clothes. Hot. Sweaty. Tired. Miserable. Mosquitoes. Leeches. Then when we were out of food and water, that was all I could think about. But when we started up that hill and those mortars started landing, I was sure I was gonna die. Now I can't get yesterday out of my mind. It's no longer important that I'm filthy and tired. I'm alive. Hell, I'm not even wounded."

"Tomorrow we'll get outta here."

"Ya really think so?'

"You gotta think so. We WILL make it."

"Thanks, Fabe. I'd never make it if you weren't here."

"Sure you would." Fabe smiled and walked back to his foxhole.

Hawk surveyed his company. Next to him was the mortar platoon. They had lost over half of their men. JR was overseeing the seven remaining men. The mortar tube and recoilless were out of commission. The first platoon was down to fourteen men. The second platoon had fared a little better. They still had sixteen. Third platoon had only ten men left.

The men had thrown the items they could not carry into an empty foxhole. They had put some C4 in the hole and burned it. Now they were burying the charred remains.

Hawk knew it would be a long night. No one would sleep. After all, they'd been in the field for seven days. They'd made very little progress. They'd had so many casualties. Now they were supposed to fight their way out with just a few men left. *Ya. We're going to fight our way out with less than half our company left. It hasn't worked so far. What are our chances of making it?*

Fabe laid on the ground next to the foxhole. He knew he wasn't going to sleep tonight, so there was no reason to sit cramped up in the hole. Fabe longed for a cigarette, but since it was dark out, that was out of the question. Brian was keeping watch. He studied Brian. He was a helluva good friend. He wished he could be as optimistic as he was. "Whatcha thinkin' about?"

"It's Sunday. Right about now, back in the world, church is getting out. After church my mom would always make a big Sunday dinner."

"If you're thinking about church, I bet you're thinking about that girl. What's her name? Susie?"

"Sara. She might'a crossed my mind."

"Think she'll go out with you when you get back?"

"A man can always dream."

"Hell, she'd be a fool to turn ya down."

"In her last letter she said she's been going out with another guy."

"So? What'd you expect her to do? Just sit home for a year?"

"I'm just saying that she'll probably be involved with someone else."

"Aw, come on. She's just playing the field."

"Maybe." Brian was glad to have someone to talk to. The night shadows played with one's imagination. Eventually your mind would play tricks on you. Talking to someone helped keep you fresh. "You think we'll get through the night without any action?"

"I hope so. We're so close to getting outta here."

"They surely know there aren't many of us left. I can't believe they won't take advantage of that."

"What happened to your "glass is half full" shit?"

Brian chuckled. "Funny, isn't it? You actually have a more positive attitude than I do."

"Damn right. I'm turning over a new leaf."

"Must be that Bible reading you did this afternoon."

CHAPTER 20

Drawing Straws

10 March 1969 – 0600 Hours

The men were already up and preparing to move out. Captain Hawk was as surprised as anybody that they had an uneventful night. He called the platoon and squad leaders together.

"I spoke to TOC. Alpha company was successfully evacuated yesterday afternoon. Both Alpha and Delta are already on Baldy. Bravo should be picked up in a couple of hours. So far everything is going as planned." He pulled out the map and spread it on the ground, pointing to where they were heading. He had shown them yesterday, but he wanted to be clear. They needed to know exactly where they were going. "Second platoon, I want you to take the lead. Next will be the first platoon and mortars. Third platoon will be last. Everyone keep alert. Because everyone is carrying extra, we'll be stopping frequently. It would only take us about an hour and a half under normal circumstances, but today I expect it will take us at least three hours. The plan is to pick us up around noon, so we can afford to pace ourselves. Once we're at our destination they will give us a more specific time. Let's get ready to roll."

At 0700 hours they entered the jungle. Brooklyn was last in the mortar platoon. JR was several people ahead. The eerie silence set Brooklyn's nerves on edge. He was carrying two M16 rifles. One he had slung over his shoulder by the strap, the other he carried in his right arm ready to fire at the slightest provocation. He watched the man ahead of him. Usually, he followed Chief or Deadeye. But they were gone. He couldn't keep his mind off the mortar attack on the hill. In his mind's eye he saw Dan and Amos blown apart. That's what happened the last time they'd tried to move forward. Now they were moving into unfamiliar territory. *Is the NVA waiting for us again? Bravo started out this same way. Maybe they expected us to follow 'em. We could be walking into a trap, just like on the hill.*

He studied his surroundings. Everything seemed to be in order. But then again, the NVA could easily stay undercover in the jungle and wait until they had Charlie Company completely surrounded. Or a single sniper could pop out of anywhere and just start picking them off. It was so damn hot! He didn't have a hand free to wipe his brow, so the sweat trickled into his eyes. His back ached from the weight of his extra load.

They had only been humping for forty minutes when they came to a clearing. Captain Hawk gave them a twenty-minute break.

Brooklyn sat beside JR. "Well, we made it this far. The rest of the way is not as dense. It should be easier going."

"As we get fartha outta the jungle, the easiuh it will be for the NVA tuh ambush us or even send in mawhtas."

"Maybe. They could have hit us hard last night, too. But they didn't."

Clark sat next to Hawk. He flicked the ashes off his cigarette. "So far, so good."

"Yes. Since Alpha made it, I have hopes for us."

"Did they say how many were left in Alpha?"

"I got the impression there were about thirty-five. It's a miracle they got outta there."

"It'll take a miracle to get us out in one piece, too."

"Do you believe in miracles, Clark?"

"I sure as hell do."

"So do I."

As JR predicted, the jungle was much easier to navigate

when they moved on at 0800 hours. The sunlight shone through the trees, making it easy to follow the person ahead.

Lil' Bro followed Merdis. Because he didn't have to concentrate so hard on the jungle terrain, his mind began wandering. If all went as planned, they'd soon be safely on a LZ. It would feel so good taking a shower, even if it was just water trickling out of a tank. The weather had been hot, so the water would be nice and warm. They'd issue him new fatigues. Maybe serve a hot meal. And he'd get mail. He'd probably have several letters from Cindy waiting for him. It sure would be nice if she sent some pictures of the baby. He might be old enough to smile and coo. He had asked Cindy to send Kool-Aid and chewing gum. Maybe she'd even send some cookies. He sure missed her. He didn't know how he was going to wait another ten months to see her without going crazy. Eventually, he'd get a leave to go on R & R. Most married men went to Hawaii so their wives could meet them there. But, even if he went to Hawaii, she'd never be able to afford to fly to Hawaii with a baby.

At 0830 hours they came to a clearing. Hawk again let them rest for twenty minutes.

Fabe sat down his rifles and dropped his rucksack on the ground. He lit a cigarette and sat down by Brian. "Feels damn good to sit down. The extra rifle and ammo sure make a difference."

"It sure is quiet."

"It sure as hell is. Too quiet."

"I guess that beats the alternative."

"Yup. As long as it stays that way."

Lil' Bro was sitting on the other side of Brian. "How much farther do we have to go?"

"Merdis said it was about three hours. So, I'd say we're about half way."

"Three hours walking? Or does that include breaks?"

"I think it includes breaks. What do you think, Fabe?"

"I'd say three hours total… As long as the gooks leave us alone."

"I got a feeling we're gonna make it without so much as a single bullet fired."

"You really think that's possible?"

"Sure, I do." Brian sounded confident.

Fabe smiled. "I guess you're back to "the cup's half full" theory."

"I sure am. God is with us. I can feel it."

As they continued on, the vegetation didn't change much. At 0925 hours, Hawk called for break. This time they only took fifteen minutes. Merdis sat down beside Lil' Bro and Fabe. "The next time we stop we'll be at our destination."

Lil' Bro smiled. "I didn't think we'd make it without an ambush of some kind."

"We're not there, yet." Fabe blew out the smoke from his cigarette.

"But we're getting close. We might just make it."

At 1005 hours they came to a grassy clearing. It was easily large enough for two helicopters to land at a time. Captain Hawk smiled as he turned to his men. "We made it. Stay at the edge of the clearing. Be sure every platoon has several men keeping watch. We don't want anyone sneaking up on us. I'll call TOC and report our progress."

After Hawk placed the call to TOC, he met with the remaining squad and platoon leaders. "Bravo got out this morning, as planned, without incident. They will pick us up in about an hour. They will be coming in three waves. Two choppers will land at a time. We need to decide who goes first and who goes last."

Clark was the first to speak up. "I think the platoon and squad leaders should go last."

"There are a few guys with us who took some shrapnel. Shouldn't they go first?" Merdis said.

Everyone began talking at once. No one wanted to go first and leave their comrades behind, but no one wanted to go last, either.

"QUIET! We're just wasting time." Hawk knew they needed to decide quickly.

JR spoke up. "How about drawing straws?"

"I like that. Let's take a vote. Who's in favor of drawing straws?"

Everyone was in agreement.

Hawk gave out the orders. "Turner, get some stalks of grass. Enough for each person. Except me. I'll go with the last group. Divide them equally; short, medium, and long. Those who get the long straw go first. Medium second, and short last."

Merdis counted the men to be sure they had the right amount of "straws". He helped Clark collect stalks of grass and break it off into three lengths.

After Clark had collected the grass, Hawk got the attention of the men. "We will be picked up in three waves. We're gonna draw straws to see who goes on each wave. Long straw goes on the first choppers out. Medium will go on the next wave. Short straw goes last. Turner will go down the line. Pick a piece of grass from his hand."

Before Clark started, Mex asked, "How many on each wave?"

"Sixteen on the first two waves. Fifteen on the last wave."

Clark stepped up to the man at the end of the group. He drew a long straw. "First."

The next man drew a short straw. "Last."

By the time he came to Brian at least half the long straws had been drawn. Brian held his breath. "Last." Brian broke out in a sweat.

Next was Fabe. "Last."

Then Mex. "First."

Lil' Bro. "Second."

JR was farther down the line. "First."

Brooklyn. "Last."

After all the men had drawn, Clark turned toward Merdis. "There's only two left. One is short. I'll take that."

"No. Let me draw just like everyone else." Merdis grabbed a stalk of grass from Clark's hand.

"That leaves me last. Just the way I wanted it." Clark turned and walked away before Merdis could argue.

Captain Hawk looked at his men. "I'm proud of all of you. You've done a great job. Now get in groups according to which wave you're on. Those on the last wave, keep a close watch on the perimeter.

It was 1104 hours when the first choppers came into sight. There were no gunships along. Their only protection was the door gunners.

Hawk looked at the first group. "Get lined up. Get the hell outta here!"

At 1107 hours Mex and JR were on their way with fourteen other men. They would be taken to LZ Professional, where a Chinook was waiting to take the whole company to LZ Baldy.

The men left behind were scared beyond belief. Only thirty-one men remained. If the NVA attacked, they would put up a fight. At least they had plenty of weapons and ammo.

Merdis sat next to Lil' Bro. "Be ready to grab your stuff when you hear the chopper in the distance. We want to board as fast as possible."

"I got it." He looked over at Fabe sitting by the last group to go out. "What about Fabe? You think he'll make it?"

Merdis lied. "Sure." He knew that each group had a significantly worse chance of making it. Even though the NVA hadn't ambushed them on the way here, they would surely see the choppers landing. He'd be surprised if they made it out without getting enemy fire. The last group had a slim chance of getting out alive.

"Won't the NVA see the choppers coming in?"

"Maybe." Merdis gave Lil' Bro a smile. "It'll sure be good to get a night's sleep for a change."

Lil' Bro knew Merdis was changing the subject because he didn't want to tell him the truth. He swallowed hard as he realized his best buddy might not make it back. He looked at Fabe again, blinking back tears. Fabe returned his look and gave him a smile and a nod. He knew Fabe was trying to tell him it was okay. But it wasn't. Nothing in this fuckin' war was okay.

Merdis could see that Lil' Bro was upset about leaving Fabe behind. "Look, Bro. You gotta take things as they come. There's no choice. You just follow orders. No point in dwelling on things you can't change. Fabe can take care of himself."

Lil' Bro hung his head and closed his eyes. He'd seen men lose their buddies. Seen them blown all to hell. He'd encountered more tragedy in the last few days than he had in his entire lifetime. Hell, most people back in the world would never see that much, no matter how old they lived to be.

He looked around at the others waiting. Praying. Hoping. Would they really make it out? He thought about the last night they were on LZ Professional. So much had changed since then. He thought about the men in the first platoon that were singing in harmony. What were their names? Harris, CJ and... what was the other guy's name? Oh yes, Ferg. They were singing "We gotta get outta this place, if it's the last thing we ever do." For CJ it was the last thing he ever did. And the other two were outta this place, too. They would be heading home soon. So many of the first platoon were gone, either wounded or killed.

He remembered the mortar platoon playing cards. How many of them were wounded or killed? He didn't even know. It was way too many.

He knew things would never be the same for him. He thought about the week he'd spent with his wife and son before he left for Nam. He thought it was tough getting up at night to feed the baby. Hell, that was nothing. He'd sat in a soft chair snuggling a warm bundle in his arms. Then he crawled back in bed beside his wife. A nice, soft, warm bed with a beautiful woman. Now he was stuck here. He had no choice. It didn't matter if they slept on the ground – or if they didn't sleep at all. It didn't matter if it was a hundred degrees and they were out of water. It didn't matter if their clothes stunk like rubbish and were stiff from the mud and blood. They had no choice except to go where and when they were ordered. And now they had no choice but to sit here and wait knowing that the NVA could attack at any minute.

Twenty minutes later Lil' Bro was sitting by the door of the chopper as it lifted off. He looked down at Fabe. Fabe waved at him. He couldn't stop a tear from trickling down his cheek. It was possible he'd never see Fabe again.

Fabe lit a cigarette. It would be another twenty minutes before the helicopters returned. A lot could happen in twenty minutes. He was glad that Lil' Bro and Merdis got out. He looked around. There were only fifteen men left. If the NVA showed up, they wouldn't stand a chance. They had certainly seen the choppers coming in. There was nothing to do but wait. And pray.

He looked at Brian. His eyes were shut, and he could tell he was praying. If they made it out, it would surely be a miracle. There was no doubt about that.

Fabe knew Charlie Company would not be sent on another mission for a couple of weeks, maybe longer. It would take a while to get in enough new men to replace all they'd lost.

Brooklyn was sitting by Clark. They both had cigarettes dangling from their mouths. Everyone was silent, as if the sound of a voice might put them over the edge. Brooklyn looked at his watch. Eleven thirty. Only five minutes had passed since the choppers took off. It seemed like at least an hour. He was sweating, but not from the heat. He took a swig of water. This had been a horrible mission. The worst he'd been on since he'd arrived in Nam last June. It was also the first time that the mortar platoon had been hit hard. God, how long before that chopper came back? He looked at his watch again. Eleven thirty-one. Maybe they'd be faster getting back this trip. They surely realized the danger the last group was in. He stared at the horizon. The sky was blue with scattered billowy clouds. It looked deceptively peaceful. Certainly not like it was in the middle of a war. He checked his watch. Eleven thirty-three. Twelve minutes until their scheduled time to return.

Clark was watching Brooklyn out of the corner of his eye. "Will you quit checking your damn watch? It's not going to make them come any sooner."

Brooklyn took a deep breath. "I know. It's just so hard waitin', okay? I expect the fuckin' NVA tuh attack any minute now. I don't know how long we can just sit here and expect them tuh leave us alone."

Clark looked at the other guys who were waiting with them. "You're not the only one. Everyone's on edge."

"How can yuh help it? We're basically helpless."

Brian checked his watch. "They should be back in another ten minutes."

Fabe took out another cigarette. He knew he was chain-smoking, but he couldn't help it. "A lot can happen in ten minutes."

"They've had plenty of chances to wipe us out. I figure if they haven't attacked yet, they're not going to."

"I sure as hell hope you're right."

"Me, too."

Brian lifted his rifle. "I saw something move."

Fabe quickly raised his rifle. He could hear his heart

pounding in his ears. His eyes searched for the slightest movement. "Where?"

Everyone followed their lead and raised their weapons, expecting an attack.

"Over there." He pointed to where the second group of men had been waiting only a short time ago. Everyone stared in that direction.

"There! That's it!" A gust of wind lifted a piece of paper out of the grass. It flitted along until it caught on another clump of grass.

Fabe could hear everyone let out a breath of relief as the paper moved. They lowered their rifles.

"My God, I thought I was going to have a heart attack." Fabe slowly lowered his rifle.

"It's no wonder, the way you've been smoking those cigarettes."

Eight minutes later the choppers appeared on the horizon. Hawk stared in disbelief. "This is it, men! Let's get the hell outta here!"

Everyone jumped up and grabbed their gear.

"Thank God." Brian was standing next to Fabe.

"You can say that again."

"We're really gonna make it."

"Don't count your chickens yet. Until we're on the choppers and in the sky, anything can happen."

"No. God will get us outta here. I can feel it."

When the men heard the rhythmic thwop-thwop of the helicopter blades in the distance, they grabbed their gear and ran to line up where the two choppers would be landing. As the choppers hovered two feet off the ground, the men wasted no time climbing on. Hawk and Clark held back to board last. As Brian hopped on the right side of the chopper Brooklyn looked around, still expecting an attack. Seeing no threats, he threw his gear in and jumped on, sitting beside Brian. Fabe stepped up to the left side of the chopper. He was almost dizzy with excitement. The thrill of boarding the chopper took his breath away. Behind him Clark and Hawk were guarding the rear. When Clark boarded, Fabe realized that they were actually going to get out.

With one last look around, Hawk made sure everyone else was safely loaded and they were in no imminent danger. In one lunge he thrust himself onto the chopper. He had barely sat down when the chopper lifted off.

After they were up in the air and nearing LZ Professional, Hawk smiled at his men. "It's a miracle."

The men all started talking at once, even though no one could hear above the sound of the chopper blades.

Eight minutes later, they landed on Professional where the rest of Charlie Company waited. Everyone cheered. Lil' Bro ran over to Fabe. "Thank God!"

"You made it, Lil' Bro. We both did." Fabe knew there was a good chance they'd get wounded, and possibly killed before their tour in Nam was over. But they'd made it this time.

Men were already climbing on the chinook, anxious to get as far away from the battle as they could.

Fabe grabbed Lil' Bro by the arm and started running toward the chinook. "Are you having fun yet?"

"Damn right, I am!"

THE END

Glossary

AIT — Advanced Infantry training.

AK 47 — A semi-automatic and fully automatic combat assault rifle, 7.62-mm; the basic weapon of the Communist forces. It is characterized by an explosive popping sound.

Artillery smoke — A smoke grenade used to mark the position for artillery attack. Can be thrown 35 meters by the average soldier.

Battalion Headquarters - A tactical and administrative organization. The battalion is typically commanded by a lieutenant colonel. It also has an executive officer, usually a major, and a command sergeant major. He gives the orders for several companies and has the capability to plan and conduct independent organizations.

BAN DA CHET — You are dead!

Birds — Helicopters, including medivacs, supply choppers, and gunships.

Blue Ghosts — F troop, 8th Cavalry, 123rd Avn BN. They were formed to provide Aerial Recon for the 23rd Infantry Division (Americal).

Camp Tien Phuoc - Special forces camp. First established in March 1966 to monitor communist infiltration into the Song Chang Valley. The base was located approximately 20 km southwest of Tam Kỳ and 43 km northwest of Chu Lai.

Charlie — North Vietnamese Army.

Cherries — A slang term for a soldier who was new and inexperienced in Vietnam.

DEROS — Date of Estimated Return from Overseas.

Didi mau — Vietnamese for go quickly.

Dink — Derogatory term for an Asian.

Door Gunner — A crewman firing manually directed armament aboard a helicopter.

Dustoff — Military term for the emergency patient evacuation of casualties from a combat zone.

FO - Forward Observer

Gooks — Derogatory term for an Asian; derived from Korean slang for "person" and passed down by Korean war veterans.

Kilometer — 0.62 miles.

Klick — One kilometer.

Lager — An area where they set up their night defensive perimeter.

LZ Baldy — A fire support base located Northwest of Chu Lai, Quang Nam Province in North central Vietnam. From 1967 until Jan 1970 LZ Baldy was the home for U.S. Army Company C, 23rd Medical Battalion Americal Division Republic of South Vietnam. The company also supported Graves Registration who took care of the deceased.

Military time - Military time operates on a 24-hour clock that begins at midnight which is referred to as 0000 hours, with 1:00 a.m. being 0100 hours, 2:00 a.m. being 0200 hours, etc. all the way to 11:00 p.m. being 2300 hours. Because it is a 24-hour clock, AM and PM are not used.

Madre de dios — Mother of God.

NVA — North Vietnamese Army

Regiment — three foot-soldier battalions

Battalion — 500-600 men each (The regulation strength for an infantry battaion was 800 officers and men, but casualties kept the operational numbers down.)

Punji stick — A sharpened piece of bamboo with length generally from one to two feet. After hardened by fire, it held an extremely sharp point for long periods of time. To increase their wound-potential, the points are often smeared with poison or animal excreta.

PX — Post Exchange.

Reconnaissance — (Recon) Going out into the jungle to observe for the purpose of identifying enemy activity.

RPG — Rocket-propelled grenade. A shoulder-fired anti-armor weapon that fires a high-explosive anti-tank grenade. Weighs less than 10 pounds.

R & R — Rest and Relaxation. Everyone in Vietnam was permitted one R&R during their one-year tour of duty. You had to complete 30 days in-country to be eligible.

Short — A soldier that had less than a month before he left Vietnam.

TOC — Tactical Operations Center — the location of radios and command and control personnel.

VC — Viet Cong, jungle-fighting guerrilla warriors who killed mainly through night-time ambushes and terrifying traps.

Radio codes:

Alpha 6 — Commander of Alpha company

Charlie 6 — Commander of Charlie Company

1-2 — First Platoon, Second squad

3-2 — Third Platoon, second squad

4-1 — Weapons

About the Author

Peggy Krause is the wife of a Vietnam Veteran. She met her husband, Philip, in 1970. He had just been discharged from the hospital in Fort Riley, Kansas, where he had been recovering for over a year from his injuries sustained in Vietnam. She is a wife, mother, grandmother, and great-grandmother.

She worked as a nurse for over forty years, of which thirty were spent working in a state Veteran's Home.

This is her first attempt at publishing books, although she had been involved in co-authoring many publications in medical journals.

The Vietnam Veterans she met at her husband's Charlie Company reunions touched her heart, and inspired her to publish both a novel and an accompanying book, which records the veteran's true stories. Her hope is to give back to the veterans by making others more aware of the sacrifices given by these brave men.

Printed in Great Britain
by Amazon

46075507R00128